Table of Contents

Crypto Confessions:
The Shocking 15 Stories that Changed the World

With real stories, the crypto world is explained to you

Javed Iqbal

Copyright Page

While every precaution has been taken in the preparation of this book, the publisher assumes no responsibility for errors or omissions, or for damages resulting from the use of the information contained herein.

Crypto Confessions: The Shocking 15 Stories that Changed the World

First edition. March 05, 2024.

Copyright © 2024 Javed Iqbal.

Written by Javed Iqbal.

About the Author

The book's author is a Crypto-blockchain Researcher with a Master in Business Administration. Since August 2017, he has offered high-quality writing services on various cryptocurrency and blockchain-related topics as a Level 2 seller on Fiverr.

He also worked for a few years as a Crypto-blockchain Researcher at Hance Law Firm Luxembourg. He collaborated with Professor Dr. Hance on writing and publishing several pieces of content in the same niche.

He is passionate about sharing his knowledge and insights with readers and helping them understand the complex but fascinating world of crypto-blockchain.

He has completed multiple crypto blockchain certification programs from leading institutions such as California University, Berkeley, USA, ConsenSyS Academy, USA, and Duke University, USA. These certifications demonstrate his proficiency and expertise in crypto blockchain technology fundamentals and applications.

LET'S CONNECT

1

2

3

4

5

6

1.   https://www.facebook.com/profile.php?id=61555414089773&mibextid=ZbWKwL

2.   https://www.tiktok.com/@javediqbaltiktok?_t=8jDPNDy0sBb&_r=1

3.   https://youtube.com/@Cryptoriesjaved?si=tQ23NvxgHmwZog8q

4.   https://www.linkedin.com/in/
javed-iqbal-a14212193?utm_source=share&utm_campaign=share_via&utm_content=profile&
utm_medium=android_app

5.   https://x.com/Javediqbal2024?t=z86Ed4avLhZJ1X1lNKga9Q&s=09

6.   https://www.instagram.com/javedcryptoblockchain?igsh=OGQ5ZDc2ODk2ZA==

INTRODUCTION

The world of crypto has become a reality. From the mysterious origins of Bitcoin to the innovative applications of smart contracts and its connection with modern and surprising automation, it is full of exciting stories and strange events.

This book contains fifteen (**15**) real stories providing insight into the modern technology's revolution, opportunities, difficulties, and risks.

You'll learn about real-life incidents in the history of the cryptocurrency and blockchain field, including the breakthroughs and scandals that shook the sector and its prospects in the future. These events center around visionaries, hackers, and innovators.

Whether you are a cryptocurrency enthusiast, critic, or spectator, the book has a wealth of helpful information and answers to your queries.

These are the short descriptions of the facts narrated in the stories:

Story 01: Bulgarian Crypto Queen fooled millions and disappeared with four billion dollars from the OneCoin Ponzi scheme.

Story 02: The story highlighted changing aspects of the life of crypto traders when crypto trading becomes a crypto addiction.

Story 03: On May 22, 2010, Jericho sold two pizzas totalling $41 to Laszlo Hanyecz for 10,000 bitcoins. It was the first Bitcoin transaction, establishing Bitcoin Pizza Day.

Story 04: A fake lover deceives the adoptive girl on the dating app. After stealing all her inherited money, he disconnected all connections.

Story 05: Changpeng Zhao (CZ) owns the world's largest cryptocurrency exchange, Binance. His success in life began with a poker game when his friend told him about Bitcoin. He is an expert in coding. The story highlights his achievements.

Story 06: A woman hired a hitman online to kill her husband and paid him in Bitcoin. The story narrates a deadly Bitcoin transaction:

Story 07: How a poor girl became a millionaire crypto influencer. She was a health worker but learned trading skills and became a successful consultant.

Story 08: First-time American newlyweds spent the first 100 days of their marriage using bitcoins in 2013. They made a documentary film, Life on Bitcoin, for which they raised 70 thousand dollars through public donations and sponsorships. Their purpose is to make people aware of the importance of cryptographic technology, especially Bitcoin.

Story 09: MT. Gox Heist: The biggest theft in cryptocurrency history, 850,000 bitcoins were stolen from the MT Gox exchange during 2011 to 2014. The exchange announced that it had recovered 200,000 bitcoins. However, 650,000 bitcoins could not be located. Mark Karpeles, the owner of the company promised to pay the cash equivalent to the worth of 200,000 bitcoins to the claimants by the end of October 2024.

Story 10: Father and son find lost bitcoins and make people rich by unlocking their wallet login passwords.

Story 11: Celebrity Kim Kardashian was fined $1.26 million. She charged for promoting the Ethereum Max token in her Instagram post. Under Kim's persuasion, people invested in the scheme and lost millions of dollars because it was a pump-and-dump scheme.

Story 12: How did the notorious hacker James Zhong create nine secret accounts and transfer over 50,000 bitcoins via 140 transactions on the dark web?

Story 13: Do Kwon's Terra Lunna Crash: The lure of huge profits lost $40 billion of investors, and the cryptocurrency market lost over $500. The TerraUST appeared as a stablecoin whose value was pegged to the dollar. Actually, Terra was not linked to the dollar but to its other cryptocurrency, LUNA. When TERRA crashed, it led to LUNA's crash as well.

CRYPTO CONFESSIONS THE SHOCKING 15 STORIES THAT CHANGED THE WORLD

Story 14: The video animator failed eight out of ten times to recover his bitcoins. If he fails two more times, he will never get any bitcoins.

Story 15: Hackers returned millions of dollars' worth of stolen cryptocurrency to a company after identifying security vulnerabilities. The company gave him the title of Mr. White hat hacker.

The moral or crux of the story is explained at the end of each story, concluding the narrative for readers.

Despite their uniqueness, these stories have fundamental importance for the crypto community. It is essential to cover these topics to understand this field.

Real-life crypto applications are explained in this book. In addition, it describes how to take advantage of it, what steps to take to protect your capital, and what risks to avoid.

Among these stories, you will find source links attached that authenticate the events mentioned. All links were sourced from highly reputable and authentic sources.

ONECOIN
PONZI SCHEME:
HOW THE BULGARIAN
CRYPTO QUEEN, DR. RUJA
IGNATOVA, FOOLED
MILLIONS
& Disappeared with 4 bn dollars?

STORY 01

5

ONECOIN PONZI SCHEME: HOW THE BULGARIAN CRYPTO QUEEN, DR. RUJA IGNATOVA, FOOLED MILLIONS AND DISAPPEARED WITH FOUR BILLION DOLLARS?

In the real story, we will tell you who the crypto queen is and why she is well known in the crypto world.

Bulgarian Dr. Ruja Ignatova (1)[1] is known as the crypto queen. She was born in Ruse, Bulgaria, on May 30, 1980. Her family moved to Germany when she was 10 years old.

She holds a Master's degree from Oxford University and a PhD from the German University of Konstanz in Private International Law.

She held a senior position at McKinney & Company, a business consulting company. In addition, she twice won the Bulgarian Businesswoman of the Year award.

Besides Bulgarian, She also spoke English and German frequently. She used to win people over with her charming conversation. She was beautiful, attractive and charismatic. She wore expensive clothes and diamond jewelry at conferences and called herself the crypto queen.

Her whereabouts have been a mystery since October 2017, and international agencies have been searching for her around the globe. She is on the FBI's 10 Most Wanted Fugitives List (2)[2].

Her partner, Karl Sebastian Greenwood, was not so lucky. In July 2018, he was arrested at his home in Koh Samui, Thailand.

According to the Police concerns, she may have undergone plastic surgery (3)[3] on her face so that no one could recognize her.

---

1.   https://en.m.wikipedia.org/wiki/Ruja_Ignatova

2.   https://nypost.com/2022/06/30/cryptoqueen-ruja-ignatova-added-to-fbis-top-ten-most-wanted-list/

3.   https://nypost.com/2023/01/28/ruja-ignatova-found-alive-after-vanishing-5-years-ago/

CRYPTO CONFESSIONS THE SHOCKING 15 STORIES THAT CHANGED THE WORLD

The story of the Bulgarian trickster is so famous that Jamie Barlett, the British journalist, has been hosting the BBC podcast "The Missing Crypto Queen" since 2019, discussing Ruja Ignatova and the OneCoin fraud. In addition, Jamie has written a book called The Missing Crypto Queen, which is available through Amazon.

Why is the crypto queen on the world's top 10 most wanted list?

Crypto Queen persuaded millions of people worldwide to join her economic revolution. Greed, deception, and blind obsession comprise her story.

In 2014, she founded the fake cryptocurrency OneCoin. As a matter of fact, it was not a cryptocurrency. The Times newspaper described her scheme as the biggest scam in history.

Between 2014 and 2017, the woman stole more than four billion dollars, cheated 3.5 million people through OneCoin, and escaped. Until today, she has been hiding.

FBI included the Crypto Queen in the top 10 most wanted (4)[1] fugitive list in June 2022. It announced a $100,000 reward for information leading to the arrest of Crypto Queen. In the FBI's 73-year history, she was the 11th woman.

---

1. https://edition.cnn.com/2023/01/22/business/ruja-ignatova-cryptoqueen-fbi-most-wanted-cec/index.html

How long has Ruja been missing?

Ruja became suspicious of her boyfriend's movements in 2017. She began spying on him. A source revealed to her that he was cooperating with the FBI. The moment she was informed, she boarded a Ryanair flight from Bulgaria to Greece (Athens) on October 25, 2017 (4)[1], and disappeared from the world, never to be seen again.

When Roja went into hiding, his brother took over the company, and he was arrested at Los Angeles Airport in March 2019.

---

1. https://edition.cnn.com/2023/01/22/business/ruja-ignatova-cryptoqueen-fbi-most-wanted-cec/index.html

Was Onecoin a cryptocurrency?

The OneCoin currency was not a cryptocurrency. Roja and her team falsely claimed that mining servers mined the OneCoin cryptocurrency. The OneCoin was not created on the blockchain and wasn't secure by blockchain technology. Therefore, it couldn't be traded on cryptocurrency exchanges, could not be used to buy anything, and investors couldn't trace their funds. Its price was not determined by market supply and demand but rather by Ignatova and her colleagues.

However, Cryptocurrencies are virtual currencies that operate on the blockchain. It is created on the blockchain. A blockchain is a digital ledger that records currency transactions. Cryptocurrency is bought and traded on various cryptocurrency exchanges. Blockchain is based on decentralized technology, which is not under centralized control like banks. There is no middleman like banks or financial institutions in this currency exchange. The market determines its value based on supply and demand.

OneCoin was a fake currency. It had no private blockchain.

Was OneCoin a Ponzi and Pyramid Scheme?

Yes, it was a Ponzi scheme, misrepresented as cryptocurrency. A Ponzi scheme refers to a type of fraud where one party promises people high returns on an investment that appears to be risk-free. In pyramid scheme (5)[1], a small initial investment yields a substantial return.

In the OneCoin Ponzi scheme, the initial investors are paid by acquiring new investors. When the scheme reaches a point where no more investors can be found, the project is terminated, and the fraudsters get away with fraudulently taking the investor's money.

---

1. https://www.justice.gov/usao-sdny/pr/co-founder-multi-billion-dollar-cryptocurrency-pyramid-scheme-onecoin-pleads-guilty

How did Missing Queen plan the OneCoin fraud?

Ignatova founded OneCoin Limited in Bulgaria in 2014. In the early days of cryptocurrency, she launched her project at the perfect time, taking advantage of speculation. Most investors had no idea how to invest in cryptocurrencies.

Roja took advantage of this opportunity to promote spam coin as the world's leading virtual currency. She claimed that this currency would bring an economic revolution on earth and change the plight of the poor. In her speech, she proclaimed that OneCoin would defeat Bitcoin and called it the "Bitcoin Killer (6)[1]."

She used to attend big parties, wear expensive clothes, show a lavish lifestyle, and own expensive properties worldwide.

Ignatova made false offers to get huge sums of money from investors, promising them a fivefold to tenfold return with minimal risk. Ignatova enticed OneCoin to sell the bogus currency to more people by luring buyers with bigger commissions.

Thus, the company's network was spread over more than 100 countries with more than 3 million investors.

The investigation revealed in an email sent by Ignatova to the co-founder that they would flee with the proceeds of the counterfeit currency and then blame someone else.

1.	https://www.bbc.co.uk/news/stories-50435014

What was the OneCoin's sales structure?

Multi-level marketing (MLM (6)[1] was the OneCoin sales structure, where investors earned a commission by selling OneCoin packages to new recruits. Likewise, if a new (recruited) investor sold a OneCoin package, he would earn a commission, as would the person who recruited him. The company sold packages worth 500, 1000, 2000, and 10,000 dollars. All investors could log in to their OneCoin accounts and see the value of their coins, which kept growing.

In a BBC podcast, The Missing Crypto Queen, Jamie Barlett talked to a victimized woman who met Roja through a Webinar hosted by the Economist.

According to the woman narrating her story, Ignatova was a very charismatic personality, and she called OneCoin the currency of the future. Initially, the woman invested 1000 dollars and immediately made a profit. As a result, she invested twelve thousand euros of his father's inheritance. Apart from this, her friend had no savings, so she got a small loan to invest in the plan. She asked many of her family friends to invest in OneCoin, and a total of 250,000 euros was invested. As a result, she is very ashamed of herself, and when she remembers all this, she is overwhelmed by how she trusted the OneCoin scam and how many people lost money because of her.

---

1. https://www.bbc.co.uk/news/stories-50435014

What steps did the FBI take to arrest Ignatova?

Investigative agencies around the world have continued to search for repentance. First, the United States issued an arrest warrant for Ignatova in 2017. In this regard, her founding partner was arrested, and her co-partner, ex-boyfriend, and lawyer were convicted. The FBI added Roja to its list of 10 most wanted fugitives.

What are the charges against Dr Roja, and how many years can he be punished?

In October 2017, the US Department of Justice Ruja Ignatova pleaded guilty to multiple charges.

Founder and leader of OneCoin, Ruja Ignatova, defrauded investors of more than $4 billion.The US Department of Justice found her guilty of multiple charges, including wire fraud, securities fraud, money laundering, and conspiracy.

She has been on the run since October 2017 and has not been captured. The FBI has listed her as one of its most wanted fugitives. If convicted, she could face prison of up to 90 years.

Has Ruja's brother been sentenced?

After the Bulgarian Queen's disappearance, the company was taken over by his brother, Konstantin Ignatova, who was arrested at Los Angeles Airport in March 2019. He was found guilty (7)[1] in November 2019 of fraud and money laundering. The US authorities signed a plea deal with him, and he agreed to cooperate with the investigation. For his fraud involvement (8)[2], he could face up to 90 years in prison. Several times, Konstantin's sentence has been scheduled, but he has not yet been sentenced, but soon he will be punished.

---

1. https://www.bbc.com/news/technology-50417908

2. https://www.justice.gov/usao-sdny/pr/manhattan-us-attorney-announces-charges-against-leaders-onecoin-multibillion-dollar

What were the charges against the co-founder of OneCoin, and what was his punishment?

U.S. Attorney's Office, District of New York, issued a press release (09)[1] on December 16, 2022, informing the public that Karl Sebastian Greenwood, 46, dual citizen status of Sweden and UK, had pleaded guilty to wire fraud, wire fraud conspiracy, and money laundering charges. The man admitted hyping (10)[2] OneCoin as a competitor to Bitcoin despite knowing that it was a fraudulent currency whose value was set arbitrarily by its backers, not by the market. He has been detained in the United States since 2018.

On September 12, 2023, the Federal Judge of New York sentenced Karl to 20 years (11)[3] in prison.

1. https://www.irs.gov/compliance/criminal-investigation/co-founder-of-multibillion-dollar-cryptocurrency-pyramid-scheme-onecoin-pleads-guilty

2. https://www.bloomberg.com/news/articles/2023-09-12/-cryptoqueen-sidekick-gets-20-years-in-4-billion-ponzi-scheme

3.   https://www.reuters.com/legal/co-founder-fake-cryptocurrency-scheme-sentenced-20-years-us-prison-2023-09-12/

How many years was Ruja's ex-boyfriend sentenced, and why?

Bloomberg Law reported on Feb. 17, 2023, that Gilbert Armenta, 59, the former boyfriend of OneCoin's founder Ruja Ignatova, had been sentenced to five years (12)[1] in prison, ordered by District Judge Edgardo Ramos, USA. Armenta helped launder $300 million in fake OneCoin investors' funds. He was convicted in 2018 of conspiring to commit wire fraud, money laundering, and extortion-related $4 billion multilevel marketing scam OneCoin. For two years, he cooperated with prosecutors in unwinding the fraud but then committed new crimes, resulting in a longer prison sentence by the government.

---

1. https://news.bloomberglaw.com/crypto/crypto-queen-boyfriend-gets-five-years-for-role-in-onecoin-scam

What is the last & latest information about missing Ignatova so far?

On February 17, 2023, the Bulgarian police published a document on their site BIRD (13)[1] in which they revealed that the former Bulgarian police chief, Mikhail Naumov, was shot dead at his residence on March 25, 2022. According to the documents found in his house during the investigation, Ruja Ignatova was ordered to be killed by Christophros Amanatidis-Taki, Crime Don of Bulgaria, in 2018. He gave this order when he was traveling in a yacht to Cuba and was intoxicated. According to Taki, Ignatova was killed and dismembered in November 2018 on another yacht in the Ionian Sea. Taki told this to the head of the Homicide department at the State Criminal Investigation, Mikhail Naumov, who was backing Taki's group.

But this was refuted by renowned journalist Atanas Tchobanov, who had worked for BIRD. According to his sources, the person who is in a relationship with Ignatova's brother said that after the rumor of Ignatova's murder, Roja contacted his brother in 2019. In addition, the investigative reporter said that in January 2023, Roja offered $13 million for the sale of her four-bedroom penthouse (14)[2] in London, which is being sold by the German authorities, which gives evidence of her survival.

According to BBC, a 13.5 (15)[3] million euro or 14.31 million US dollars apartment in Kensington, London, which was owned by Ruja Ignatova, the infamous Onecoin scammer who disappeared in 2017, was listed for sale in January 2023. Bielefeld's prosecutor accused Ignatova's German lawyer, Martin Breidenbach, of laundering money for transferring €20 million to purchase the Kensington penthouse

---

1. https://bird.bg/ruja-ignatova-taki/

2.   https://www.bbc.com/news/uk-england-london-64407723

3.   https://www.bbc.com/news/stories-59062959

and another apartment in the same building. Breidenbach denied the charge, and his trial has continued since September 2021. He remained Director of OneCoin Limited from December 2014 to December 2015. He was responsible for giving legal opinion in favor of the company that was used in promoting OneCoin. His trial (16)[4] is ongoing in a court in Munster, Germany.

---

4. https://news.bitcoin.com/onecoin-cryptoqueen-associates-appear-in-german-court/

The Moral of the Story:

It's a story of greed, deception, and blind obsession.

In 2014, Dr Ruja, a Bulgarian crypto fugitive, founded the fraudulent virtual currency OneCoin, which lacks blockchain, mining, and absolute value. She described it as a revolutionary cryptocurrency that would change your life and beat Bitcoin. From this story, we learn five lessons. First, be aware that unrealistic claims and promises are often based on lies. Bulgarian women adopted this deceptive method. Therefore, it's crucial to conduct extensive research and verify the credibility of any cryptocurrency before investing. Second, confirming that it is listed on a reputable cryptocurrency exchange is also essential.

Third, does the currency comply with the regulatory requirements? Is it a cryptocurrency or a token? Can it be classified as a currency, security, commodity, or something else?

Fourth, this story shows you shouldn't be swayed by charismatic figures who support your currency. Roja, who created the currency, was a PhD student and senior at McKinsey. Furthermore, she also received an award for being a successful businesswoman. Roja used expensive clothes, cars, and diamond jewellery. She had a charming personality that inspired many people to invest in OneCoin.

Last but not least, schemes that advertise heavily and promise unrealistic profits are actually fake schemes. One should avoid them at all costs.

References:

1. Wikipedia contributors. (n,d). *Ruja Ignatova*. Wikipedia. https://en.m.wikipedia.org/wiki/Ruja_Ignatova

2. Propper, D. (2022, June 30). "Cryptoqueen" Ruja Ignatova has been added to FBI's 10 most wanted list. *New York Post*.https://nypost.com/2022/06/30/cryptoqueen-ruja-ignatova-added-to-fbis-top-ten-most-wanted-list/

3. News.com.au. (2023, January 28). Missing 'crypto queen' Ruja Ignatova found alive after vanishing 5 years ago. *New York Post*.https://nypost.com/2023/01/28/ruja-ignatova-found-alive-after-vanishing-5-years-ago/

4. *Karimi.F.* (2023, January 22). CNN News. *This 'Cryptoqueen' scammed investors out of $4 billion, the FBI says. Then she boarded a plane and disappeared.* https://edition.cnn.com/2023/01/22/business/ruja-ignatova-cryptoqueen-fbi-most-wanted-cec/index.html

5. Press Release. DOJ. NY. (2022, December 16).*Co-Founder of Multi-Billion-Dollar cryptocurrency pyramid scheme "OneCoin" pleads guilty.*https://www.justice.gov/usao-sdny/pr/co-founder-multi-billion-dollar-cryptocurrency-pyramid-scheme-onecoin-pleads-guilty

6. BBC News. (2019, November 24). Cryptoqueen: How this woman scammed the world, then vanished. *BBC News*.https://www.bbc.co.uk/news/stories-50435014

7. BBC News. (2019, November 14). "Cryptoqueen" brother admits role in OneCoin fraud. *BBC News*.https://www.bbc.com/news/technology-50417908

8. *Press Release. DOJ NYK.* (2020, April 30).*Manhattan U.S. attorney announces charges against leaders of "OneCoin," a Multibillion-Dollar pyramid scheme involving the sale of a fraudulent cryptocurrency.*https://www.justice.gov/usao-sdny/pr/manhattan-us-attorney-announces-charges-against-leaders-onecoin-multibillion-dollar

9. IRS.gov. (2022, Dec. 16).*Co-founder of multibillion-dollar cryptocurrency pyramid scheme "OneCoin" pleads guilty | Internal Revenue Service.*https://www.irs.gov/compliance/criminal-investigation/co-

founder-of-multibillion-dollar-cryptocurrency-pyramid-scheme-onecoin-pleads-guilty

10. Van Voris, B., & Yang, Y. (2023, September 12). 'Cryptoqueen' sidekick Karl Sebastian Greenwood gets 20 years in ponzi scheme. *Bloomberg.com*.https://www.bloomberg.com/news/articles/2023-09-12/-cryptoqueen-sidekick-gets-20-years-in-4-billion-ponzi-scheme

11. Singh. K., & Godoy. J. (2023, September 13). Reuters.*Co-founder of fake cryptocurrency scheme sentenced to 20 years in US prison*.https://www.reuters.com/legal/co-founder-fake-cryptocurrency-scheme-sentenced-20-years-us-prison-2023-09-12/

12. Van Voris, B. (2023, February 17). 'Cryptoqueen' Boyfriend Gets Five Years in OneCoin Scam (1). *BLOOMBERG*.https://news.bloomberglaw.com/crypto/crypto-queen-boyfriend-gets-five-years-for-role-in-onecoin-scam

13. Stoyanov, D., & Tchobanov, A. (2023, Feb. 17). Information in the Ministry of the Interior: Ruzha Ignatova was killed on the order of Taki. The head of Homicide worked for him. BIRD.https://bird.bg/ruja-ignatova-taki/

14. Byrne. R. & Bartlett. J. (2023, January 27). Cryptoqueen: Has the missing fugitive reappeared? *BBC News*.https://www.bbc.com/news/uk-england-london-64407723

15. BBC News. (2021, November 3). Revealed: The Cryptoqueen's £13.5m London penthouse. *BBC News*.https://www.bbc.com/news/stories-59062959

16. Tassev, L. (2022, October 21). *Onecoin Cryptoqueen associates appear in German court*. Bitcoin News.https://news.bitcoin.com/onecoin-cryptoqueen-associates-appear-in-german-court/

CRYPTORIES WITH JAVED
A STORY OF
3 LIVES
HOW DOES CRYPTO TRADING BECOME AN ADDICTION?

STORY 02

HOW DOES CRYPTO TRADING BECOME AN ADDICTION? A STORY OF THREE LIVES

We often hear that Bitcoin traders are making money, but we don't hear that they also lose money daily. The story (1)[1] illustrates how cryptocurrency trading has affected the lives of individuals who are addicted to it.

A Scottish Tony Marini runs a clinic in Scotland, UK, that has treated hundreds of people who have lost everything in cryptocurrency gambling.

According to Tony, cryptocurrency has the same status in crypto trading as cocaine has in gambling.

Jack is one of those who lost everything in virtual currency. He is from Scotland. In 2015, he bought bitcoins. A few years later, when the value of Bitcoin increased significantly, Jack had a huge success.

As Jack's interest in cryptocurrency trading grew, he became addicted. There was a time when he lost everything. He was so addicted to coin trading that one day, he lost millions of pounds that weren't his money in just a 20-minute trade because the market was so bullish.

He was responsible for safeguarding millions of pounds in the company he had invested in crypto trading. He lost his own money and the company's large sums in cryptocurrency trading addiction.

His relatives managed to pay the company 15 million pounds with great difficulty. After that, he sought treatment at Tony's clinic.

In Tony's opinion, it's like the cocaine of the gambling world that people have easy access to. A market with such extreme volatility can make people break in just a few moments.

---

1. https://www.bbc.com/news/uk-scotland-57268024

Jane Mac, another victim of crypto addiction, lost more than two and a half million euros in trading. This amount also includes money from his friends and family members.

Jane says it is more important to know the risks associated with this technology before using it.

Further, she recommended that people who are unfamiliar with it first understand it or seek expert advice. In any other case, investing in it would be a gamble. Ultimately, regret is the result.

How do crypto addicts lose their capital?

Trading cryptocurrency and its technology is complex. Many people invest in this technology for the lure of wealth without understanding it and end up losing their lifetime earnings.

Investing in bot trading without understanding it is a waste of money. When to use stop loss and stop profit techniques, when to sell the coin, and when to buy it. Before trading in crypto, it's essential to know all this.

Also, users should be aware that Ethereum or other coins held in Defi staking may decrease in value at any time during a bear market.

Does this happen to all crypto trading users?

In fact, no. It doesn't happen to everyone. Cameron Black is a freelance musician; the lockdown severely affected his income. His concerts ended, and he became housebound. As soon as he saw the crypto market start to pick up in March 2020, he invested in it and became very successful. Despite adverse Crona circumstances, he has succeeded and is satisfied with his investment.

The Moral of the Story:

Crypto trading is like a drug addiction. Getting ahead in this field is only possible in two ways.

Firstly, you must be familiar with cryptocurrencies and trading methods.

If you are involved in day trading, you should know the virtual currency's price on different exchanges. Otherwise, hire experts and make sure they are qualified.

Secondly, it is essential to control your emotions. People invest more money when they lose money in the hope that they will recover their losses. During these situations, they commit mistakes that cause irreparable damage to themselves in minutes.

Exiting the market after losing 3-5% of your total capital is advisable, mainly when the market is fast. Wait for the market until the bearish trend breaks.

References:

1. Peters, J. (2021, May 29). "I lost millions through cryptocurrency trading addiction." *BBC News*. https://www.bbc.com/news/uk-scotland-57268024

CRYPTORIES WITH JAVED
THE ORIGINS OF BITCOIN PIZZA DAY
THE STORY BEHIND THE WORLD'S FIRST BITCOIN TRANSACTION!

STORY 03

33

THE ORIGINS OF BITCOIN PIZZA DAY: THE STORY BEHIND THE WORLD'S FIRST BITCOIN TRANSACTION

On this historic day, the first Bitcoin transaction took place. Bitcoin was used for the first time to purchase goods, making it famous deal.

Computer programmer Laszlo Hanyecz announced an offer on Tuesday, May 18, 2010, that he would give 10,000 bitcoins to a person who gives him two large pizzas.

Previously, Bitcoin was not used for buying and selling. That day, Laszlo told his children they would eat pizza instead of a home-cooked dinner.

The New York Times (1)[1] popularized this odd offer for the first time in 2013, and later tweeted by @Bitcoin (2)[2] Tweeter handle in 2014.

---

1. https://archive.nytimes.com/bits.blogs.nytimes.com/2013/12/22/disruptions-betting-on-bitcoin/

2. https://twitter.com/bitcoin/status/469380926443896833?lang=en

How did he offer 10000 bitcoins for two pizzas?

On May 18, 2010, in a post on the bitcointalk.org forum (3)[1], Laszlo Hanyecz said,

"I'll pay 10,000 bitcoins for a couple of pizzas.. like maybe 2 large ones, so I have some leftover for the next day. I like having leftover pizza to nibble on later. You can make the pizza yourself and bring it to my house or order it for me from a delivery place, but what I'm aiming for is getting food delivered in exchange for bitcoins where I don't have to order or prepare it myself, kind of like ordering a 'breakfast platter' at a hotel or something, they just bring you something to eat, and you're happy!"

He expressed his desire to exchange 10,000 bitcoins for two pizzas. He said he preferred to avoid cooking or ordering food himself. He wanted someone to bring me pizza or order them for me and make me happy.

Three days passed, but no one accepted the pizza offer in exchange for bitcoins. One of the reasons was that Bitcoin was undervalued at the time. Bitcoin was less than a dollar.

He wrote:

"So no one wants to buy me a pizza? Is the amount of Bitcoin I'm offering too low?"

In 2010, it cost about .004 (4)[2]cents. It had a very low value and was not traded on any exchange.

---

1. https://bitcointalk.org/index.php?topic=137.msg1181#msg1181

2.   https://buybitcoinworldwide.com/price/#a5c02393e59c943d6a75a9241140faca32010

When and how was the deal finalized?

Finally, on May 22, 2010 (3)[1], nineteen-year-old student Jeremy "Jerkos" Sturdivant accepted Laszlo's offer. He bought two large pizzas for $41 and delivered them to his home. In exchange for pizza, he received 10,000 bitcoins.

Laszlo mined these bitcoins using computer graphics cards.

On Saturday, May 22, 2010, at 7:17:26 seconds, Laszlo mentioned this on the Bitcoin Talk forum and said:

"I just want to report that I successfully traded 10,000 bitcoins for pizza. Thanks jerkos!"

Furthermore, he posted two photos showing two large pizzas in Papa John's franchise boxes. In the second picture, he is at the dinner table with his son and daughter with pizza.

---

1. https://bitcointalk.org/index.php?topic=137.msg1181#msg1181

How did people react to Laszlo's offer of 10,000 bitcoins for two large pizzas?

Many people (3)[1] found the offer odd. A forum user said Hanyecz could sell 10,000 BTC for $41 right now instead of just exchanging food, which he could order directly and pay with dollars like any other pizza lover.

Another user asked, "Are you hungry, or do you like pizza?"

In response, Laszlo explained the purpose of his transaction, saying:

It would be interesting if I could say I paid for a pizza in bitcoins."

Jeremy "Jirkos" Sturdivant eventually accepted the offer. In a 2015 interview with the website Bitcoin Who's Who, Jerkos said that he finalized the deal with Laszlo on IRC, Internet Relay Chat. The Internet Relay Chat (IRC) is a social communication platform where people can communicate online.

---

1. https://bitcointalk.org/index.php?topic=137.msg1181#msg1181

What did Jericho reveal about his deal with Laszlo?

Jericho revealed some facts in a 2015 interview with Bitcoin Who's Who (5)[1], and he said that he gave Laszlo two large Domino's pizzas, but the photo he posted on bitcointalk.com was from Papa John's boxes.

Jerkos said he finalized the deal with Laszlo on IRC, Internet Relay Chat. He didn't have an account on bitcoin.talk.com, he could not reply.

Jericho bought amusement tickets and sold these coins when their value increased ten times to $400.

---

1. https://bitcoinwhoswho.com/index/jercosinterview

If any of them had bitcoins today?

Bitcoin's price increased to 67 thousand dollars in 2021. If any of them had 10,000 bitcoins, their total value would be more than 670 million dollars.

On December 18, 2023, one bitcoin was worth $41,600. If 10,000 bitcoins were sold, they would be worth $416 million. Both missed the chance to become millionaires.

The Moral of the Story:

In history, Hanyecz will be remembered as the first person who offered Bitcoin for sale. While Jerkos is the first teenager who bought two pizzas for $41, gave them to Laszlo, and took 10,000 bitcoins from him.

Thus, Laszlo ate the world's most expensive pizza, and Jericho bought bitcoins at the cheapest price of $.004 per bitcoin.

Unfortunately, both of them were not aware of Bitcoin's increasing value in the early days, so they used it regardless. As a result, both missed the opportunity to become billionaires.

Both are remembered in the crypto world as the first to use Bitcoin to purchase goods in the real world, making it a valuable currency.

References:

1. Bilton, N. (2013, December 22). *Disruptions: Betting on a coin with no realm*. Bits Blog. https://archive.nytimes.com/bits.blogs.nytimes.com/2013/12/22/disruptions-betting-on-bitcoin/

2. https://twitter.com/bitcoin/status/469380926443896833?lang=en

3. Bitcointalk.org. (2010, May 2018). Pizza for bitcoins. https://bitcointalk.org/index.php?topic=137.msg1181#msg1181

4. *Bitcoin Price History Chart (2009, 2010 to 2023)*. (n.d.). Buy Bitcoin Worldwide. https://buybitcoinworldwide.com/price/#2010[1]

5. *Bitcoin Address lookup, Checker and scam Reports - BitcoinWhosWho*. (n.d.). https://www.bitcoinwhoswho.com/index/jercosinterview

---

[1]. https://buybitcoinworldwide.com/price/#a5c02393e59c943d6a75a9241140faca32010

THE FAKE
LOVER CHEATS
THE ADOPTIVE
GIRL ON THE
DATING APP
CRYPTORIES
WITH
JAVED

STORY 04

43

THE FAKE LOVER CHEATS THE ADOPTIVE GIRL ON THE DATING APP

CBS News (1)[1] revealed a real story about crypto fraud with a 24-year-old woman, Nicole Hutchinson, aired on February 22, 2022.

It was reported that a young lady from the South American state of Tennessee lost $390,000 of her and her father's lifetime savings after falling victim to an online crypto-dating scam. Nicole, a foster child, inherited her mother's house, which she sold for $280,000. Hutchinson wanted to use the money to settle in California with her family.

She thought, why not make some friends before going to California? For this purpose, she started using Hinge, an online dating website where she befriended a man named Hao.

Hutchinson felt a sense of belonging with Hao when the boy told him that he came from the same town in China where she was adopted. And she began to believe his words.

Hao encouraged her to invest in cryptocurrency. The girl did not know about crypto trading. Hao told the girl this is my field, and I can be your teacher, assuring her that he would not let her money sink and that she would have a lot of profit. The girl had a true heart; she began to trust the boy because of his smooth talk.

The boy told Hutchinson to create an account on Crypto.com (2)[2], a legitimate crypto site. He sent her a link and asked Hinchinson to transfer the money to the new link.

Initially, she invested small amounts and then larger amounts. When the girl's account started showing profits, she advised her father to invest as well, and he did.

---

1. https://www.cbsnews.com/news/crypto-dating-scam/

2.   https://crypto.com/

By December 2021, their accounts showed a combined balance of $1.2 million, and Hutchinson decided it was time to cash out. That's when the site told her that before she could withdraw her money, she would have to pay a hefty "tax bill" of about $380,000.

She was very surprised to know this. When she contacted Hao, he either closed all his accounts, created new ones, or cut off all communication. She realized she had been cheated on, and her heart was bleeding.

All her and her father's funds had gone into the pockets of the fake lover. *"I messed up my life. I messed up my dad's life,"* Hutchinson said.

When she tearfully told her father about this scam, the old father also consoled his daughter with tears in his eyes and said, *"Okay, okay."*

How did the scammer transfer Hutchinson's money?

Hutchinson's money started in legitimate cryptocurrency accounts, but the links the fraudster provided to transfer the money were the scammers' own digital wallets.

Why did the girl tell the world about her fraud?

She wanted to make sure someone else's daughter or father would not lose their lifetime earnings as she did. People need to be careful when spending their money.

You should not invest in any crypto investment scheme until you are fully informed about it.

Remember, people are often cheated by what they trust.

The Moral of the Story:

For crypto users, the story has two messages.

Firstly, Fraud occurs primarily because of the user's lack of knowledge about cryptocurrency investments and inexperience.

Secondly, the important message is that friendships made on dating sites are never real friendships. Always keep your financial secrets confidential, and never trust strangers with your money.

References:

1. Werner. A. (2022, February 22). Woman loses $390,000 in online crypto dating scam: "I messed up my life."*CBS News*. https://www.cbsnews.com/news/crypto-dating-scam/

2. *Crypto.com | Securely buy, sell & trade Bitcoin, Ethereum and 250+ Altcoins.* (n.d.-c). https://crypto.com/

CRYPTORIES WITH JAVED
HOW DID THE SOFTWARE DEVELOPER BECOME THE OWNER OF THE WORLD'S LARGEST CRYPTOCURRENCY EXCHANGE, BINANCE?

STORY 05

51

HOW DID THE SOFTWARE DEVELOPER BECOME THE OWNER OF THE WORLD'S LARGEST CRYPTOCURRENCY EXCHANGE, BINANCE?

We will tell you the story of a successful person whose fortune in life started with the game of poker. This is the man whose mother calls him an idiot who made burgers at McDonald's.

He quits his job to understand investing in Bitcoin and spend time in the coding process. He sold his apartment and bought Bitcoin with all the money, but after two months, he had to see a loss of up to 70% of this amount.

Then, there was a time in his life when he founded the world's largest crypto exchange, Binance, and became the wealthiest person in the crypto world in 180 days.

Changpeng Zhao (CZ) (1)[1] was born in a village in Jiangsu, China, on February 5, 1977. During his childhood, he obtained water daily from a water pump by running a tap.

In 1989, when he turned twelve, he started his life's struggle and moved to Canada. He continued his education for the next ten years, during which he spent six years in Vancouver and four years in Montreal. In his teens, he worked as a burger maker at McDonald's to support his household and completed his studies in computer science at McGill University in Montreal. He started his career in the world of software development.

He was moved to Japan for work, where he developed software for matching trade orders in the Tokyo Stock Exchange. He then moved to New York and worked for four years at Bloomberg Tradebook as a futures trading software developer.

---

1.   https://en.wikipedia.org/wiki/Changpeng_Zhao

CRYPTO CONFESSIONS THE SHOCKING 15 STORIES THAT CHANGED THE WORLD

After spending 16 years abroad, in 2005, at the age of twenty-eight, CZ returned to his native China (Shanghai). Here, he started a company called Fusion Systems along with his five friends. It was a high-frequency trading system for brokers, i.e., a trading system that analyzed the markets using algorithms and executed many orders at lightning speed. CZ was associated with this work for eight years, but then he left it.

One day in 2013, he was playing a poker game (2)[2] with his friends. One of these friends said to him do you know about Bitcoin? Zhao heard this word for the first time. He asked what it is. The friend said that it is the money of the internet for the internet. He felt great knowing about Bitcoin.

Changpeng went home and downloaded the 9-page Bitcoin white paper, starting to understand its technology well. As a developer, his interest in the currency grew as he read the paper.

Thus, in his 36 years of life, he started learning about blockchain-based technology. He used to go to different conferences. In December 2013, he attended a conference in Las Vegas that only 200 people attended. He got the opportunity to listen to the prominent figures related to crypto at this conference, including Charlie, the inventor of Litecoin, and Vitalik, the inventor of the popular Ethereum.

Here, Zaho met a guy who told him how to transfer the Ripple currency from one wallet account to another. This guy transferred Ripple to CZ. Zhao said I would return this Ripple currency to your wallet account, but the boy said no, you should share it to teach someone else.

Chanpeng explains that the value of these ripples was equivalent to 500 dollars, which was not a large amount, but not so small either. He

---

2.   https://www.bloomberg.com/news/features/2022-01-09/binance-ceo-cz-s-net-worth-billionaire-holds-world-s-biggest-crypto-fortune?leadSource=uverify%20wall

was impressed by the man's attitude and the crypto community behind the technology. So, after returning from the conference, he

sold his house, which netted him ten million dollars. With all this money, he bought Bitcoin.

Zhao sold his house and bought bitcoins for $600 each, but unfortunately, after two months, their price dropped from $600 to $200, which did not rise for another two years. He had to bear the burden of loss of up to 70% of his money.

CZ did not care about this loss and even quit his job so that he could devote his full time to blockchain technology and coding.

His friends thought he was crazy; even his mother used to say, Zhao, you are a stupid person to have lost so much money. Why don't you get a job in a good company?

Why wasn't Changpeng Zhao upset about these problems?

Changpeng believed that blockchain is tomorrow's technology; he considered Bitcoin the money of the future. He was so firm in his belief that he continued his struggle and did not waver even in the most challenging situations.

For the next four to five years, he worked day and night. He used to work from 9 am till night. He stopped seeing all his friends, said goodbye to his favorite poker game, and threw himself into work.

When did Zhao establish the Binance Crypto exchange?

Zhao dabbled in coding, and in 2017, when he turned 40, he founded the cryptocurrency exchange Binance. His mission was that Binance would be one of the ten largest cryptocurrency exchanges in the coming three years, but in just six months, i.e., 180 days (3)[1], Binance cryptocurrency exchange rose to the top position.

---

1. https://www.binance.com/en/blog/from-cz/from-burgers-to-bitcoin-billions-how-cz-built-a-leading-crypto-exchange-in-just-180-days-421499824684901276

When did CZ's success begin?

The five-year period from 2017 to 2022 is the time of his eternal success when he had no wealth in 2017 and became the wealthiest person in the crypto world in 2022. According to the Forbes (4)[1] Billionaire 2022 report, his personal assets are more than 65 million dollars, and he ranks 19th on the list of richest people globally. Success kissed his feet, and he never looked back.

1. https://www.forbes.com/sites/johnhyatt/2022/04/05/the-wealthiest-person-in-crypto-climbs-into-worlds-20-richest/?sh=495f0734dd19

Did he work hard to earn money?

Not at all; he is a very humble person who wears ordinary clothes and does not have big cars. He says that he did not do all these struggles to get wealth, but the purpose of his life is to do things that benefit people and affect people's lives. Changpeng says he will allocate his wealth to charity.

The Moral of the story:

The story teaches that whatever you aim for in life, whatever you do, you must have a strong conviction. You must have full confidence in your success. Zhao was a computer programmer. He had technical skills and technology expertise and put those skills to practical use in several companies. Changpeng mastered crypto-blockchain methods and coding techniques. He spent time and never looked back but solved the steps to success with his skill, dedication, and conviction. Whoever adopts these qualities will surely succeed in the practical field despite facing many difficulties.

References:

1. Wikipedia contributors. (2023, November 11). Changpeng Zhao. Wikipedia. https://en.wikipedia.org/wiki/Changpeng_Zhao

2. Maloney, T., Yang, Y., & Bartenstein, B. (2022, January 10). Binance CEO CZ's Net Worth: Billionaire Holds World's Biggest Crypto Fortune. Bloomberg.com. https://www.bloomberg.com/news/features/2022-01-09/binance-ceo-cz-s-net-worth-billionaire-holds-world-s-biggest-crypto-fortune?leadSource=uverify%20wall

3. From burgers to Bitcoin billions: How CZ built a leading crypto exchange in just 180 days | Binance Blog. (n.d.). Binance Blog. https://www.binance.com/en/blog/from-cz/from-burgers-to-bitcoin-billions-how-cz-built-a-leading-crypto-exchange-in-just-180-days-421499824684901276

4. Hyatt, J. (2022, April 5). The Wealthiest Person In Crypto Climbs Into World's 20 Richest. Forbes. https://www.forbes.com/sites/johnhyatt/2022/04/05/the-wealthiest-person-in-crypto-climbs-into-worlds-20-richest/?sh=495f0734dd19

CRYPTORIES WITH JAVED
THE DARK
SIDE OF BITCOIN:
HOW A WOMAN HIRED A
HITMAN ONLINE
TO KILL HER HUSBAND

STORY 06

THE DARK SIDE OF BITCOIN: HOW A WOMAN HIRED A HITMAN ONLINE TO KILL HER HUSBAND

Jessica Leeann Sledge, 40, from Pelahachie, Mississippi, USA, hired a Bitcoin Killer (1)[1] on the dark web to murder her husband from September 2021 to November 01, 2021.

The accused paid $10,000 in bitcoins to the assassin in three payments. The payments were made on 4, 9, and 10 October 2021. She used the internet, phone calls, and WhatsApp to communicate.

Jessica sent the pictures (2)[2] of her spouse, his car, license, and number plate to the secret invader and informed him of his daily affairs.

The hitman told the woman he had made several attempts to target her husband but failed.

The hired killer asked the woman why she wanted to murder her husband; she stated she had feelings of revenge for him. The couple was in the process of divorcing. Jessica had also been in a relationship with another person for two years. The woman expressed her intention to get married after the murder of her husband.

On October 26, Sledge contacted the secret invader on WhatsApp, informing him that her husband went to the Marathon Gas station store for breakfast in a particular Vehicle.

Once again, the plan to kill her husband failed.

Eventually, on November 1st, the woman was arrested by FBI agents in Brandon, Mississippi, for paying the hitman more cash.

---

1. https://www.wlbt.com/2022/08/01/this-is-an-egregious-case-judge-sentences-pelahatchie-woman-10-years-murder-for-hire-plot/

2. https://www.oxygen.com/crime-news/jessica-sledge-sentenced-10-years-bitcoin-murder-for-hire

Who was Bitcoin Hitman, and what happened to the woman?

The drop-scene of the story happened when it was revealed that the hitman was an FBI under covered agent. The woman searched to hire an assassin on the Dark web using Bitcoin currency to assassinate her husband, and she found an undercover FBI agent who introduced himself as a Bitcoin killer.

The woman was sued in a Mississippi court. Her actions were recognized as serious crimes. Additionally, the accused attempted to kill her husband several times.

The FBI produced numerous phone calls, messages, and payments against Jessica as substantial evidence. In addition, the accused confessed to her crime.

While giving his remarks after hearing the case, the judge said that at no point during this period did Jessica realize her mistake, nor did she change her intentions.

Sledge's attorney, Colette, argued that his client committed a crime for the first time in her life and she should be treated leniently.

Assistant U.S. Attorney David Fulcher opposed this, stating that the accused plotted the murder with a secret agent.

The judge later remarked after hearing the case he did not feel at any place that the accused was scared during a planned murder attempt, nor did she show any change in her intention.

As a result of all the evidence against her, United States Southern District Mississippi Judge Carlton W. Reeves (3)[1] sentenced her to ten years and a fine of $1,000 on August 1, 2022.

---

1.   https://www.justice.gov/usao-sdms/pr/pelahatchie-woman-sentenced-statutory-maximum-10-years-murder-hire-plot

Additionally, after her prison term, she will have to spend three years under supervision, during which she cannot even contact her ex-husband.

Has any incident of a deadly Bitcoin transaction ever occurred before?

Yes, an incident similar to this occurred in 2021 when Nelson Replogle, a Tennessee man, hired a hitman to kill his wife (4)[1] on a murder-for-hire website. He gave details about his wife's car, timing schedule, and when she would visit the veterinarian to examine her pet. As a result of obtaining the Bitcoin transaction details on Coinbase wallet, the FBI arrested the husband. Fortunately, his wife survived the murder plot.

---

1. https://decrypt.co/106454/woman-behind-bitcoin-murder-for-hire-plot-sentenced-to-ten-years-in-prison

The Moral of the story:

On the one hand, cryptocurrency is a borderless virtual currency independent of the control of a central bank or government. It preserves the privacy and freedom of the user, but on the other hand, its misuse causes dangerous consequences in society. The regulatory authorities should take steps to prevent the misuse of this currency and take advantage of its beneficial aspects.

References:

1. Warren, A. (2022, August 1). 'This is an egregious case': Judge sentences Pelahatchie woman to 10 years in murder-for-hire plot. https://www.wlbt.com/2022/08/01/this-is-an-egregious-case-judge-sentences-pelahatchie-woman-10-years-murder-for-hire-plot/

2. Johnson, C. (2022, August 2). Mississippi Woman Who Used Bitcoin To Hire Hitman To Kill Her Ex Gets 10 Years. Oxygen Official Site. https://www.oxygen.com/crime-news/jessica-sledge-sentenced-10-years-bitcoin-murder-for-hire

3. Pelahatchie Woman sentenced to statutory maximum of 10 years in Murder-For-Hire plot. (2022, August 1). https://www.justice.gov/usao-sdms/pr/pelahatchie-woman-sentenced-statutory-maximum-10-years-murder-hire-plot

4. Nelson, J. (2022, August 2). Woman behind Bitcoin murder for hire plot sentenced to ten years in prison. Decrypt. https://decrypt.co/106454/woman-behind-bitcoin-murder-for-hire-plot-sentenced-to-ten-years-in-prison

CRYPTORIES
WITH
JAVED
ETHUSD
A JOURNEY
FROM POOR
GIRL TO
MILLIONAIRE
CRYPTO
INFLUENCER

STORY 07

A JOURNEY FROM POOR GIRL TO MILLIONAIRE CRYPTO INFLUENCER

It is an inspiring story (1)[1] about a brave girl who changed her fate. Her name is WendyO.

She lives in Los Angeles, California. She created a YouTube channel called WendyOCryptO in 2018 to provide crypto education and consultancy to the public.

Aside from consulting cryptocurrency companies and promoting many projects, she earns millions of dollars just from her YouTube channel.

Her father died when she was eleven years old. She lived in extreme poverty. As a healthcare worker (2)[2], she worked in the health sector. She thought only she could be serious about her life in her difficult situation.

If anyone is worried about me, she can only worry about herself and make it good.

WendyO aimed to make her life better by changing it. There was a moment in her life that changed everything. One evening in 2017, she was driving home in her car when she returned from nursing duty. She heard on the car radio that crypto trading is becoming increasingly popular globally, especially Bitcoin. In January 2017, Bitcoin's price was 1100 dollars, but it gradually increased to 4000 dollars in September, 6500 dollars in October,10,000 dollars in November, and it had reached 20,000 dollars by the end of December 2017. Her attention was drawn to Bitcoin because of this unusual price trend.

---

1. https://cointelegraph.com/news/crypto-stories-youtuber-cryptowendyo-shares-how-her-healthcare-skills-helped-with-crypto-trading

2. https://everipedia.org/wiki/lang_en/wendy-o

She was surprised to learn how bitcoin trading can drastically change a person's life and how risky it is.

A curiosity arose in her mind about crypto coins. She began learning trading techniques and then taught people how to trade various coins profitably.

How did she start her career in crypto trading?

Wendyo invested in cryptocurrency and learned about it. She learned from YouTube, obtaining information from Google about when price levels rise, why they rise, and when they fall.

She realized that Bitcoin works on the fundamental principle of supply and demand. If more people or stakeholders trade in it, its value increases. If fewer people, investors, or large companies trade in it, its demand decreases, reducing its value.

Additionally, if the media creates hype about it, its value increases. Crypto investments are reduced when the same media reports that mining crypto increases environmental pollution.

As a crypto trader, the girl gained an understanding of when and how to make the best buys and sells.

Furthermore, the girl worked in a healthcare job as a patient counselor, where she met many people each day and communicated directly with them daily. This experience gave her ease and success in trading consultations.

She began advising and speaking to people about Bitcoin trading during her job. Several people made money from her opinions, which led her to establish her own YouTube channel, CryptoWendyo, on April 19, 2018. Her videos provide market insight, technical analysis, interviews, and project details.

She continued to succeed in this way, and now she has become one of the world's most respected, famous, and wealthy crypto trading influencers.

What kind of advice does a YouTuber give on her YouTube Cryptocurrency channel?

Crypto Wendyo on YouTube takes you inside the market. On the Cryptocurrency YouTube Influencer's channel, you can find a range of crypto interviews, reviews of crypto projects, market updates, price trends, and technical analyses.

In addition to daily and weekly Bitcoin and altcoin news, Wendyo's channel tells you about the new Bitcoin NFT trend that can make you a millionaire and which stablecoin was banned by the USA. In her channel, she discusses how Metamask wallets can be used for staking. The YouTuber also explains how malware attacks NFTs and what mistakes the crypto space should avoid. Across the globe, people follow her channel.

The Crypto YouTuber also promotes the projects of other companies. The cryptocurrency influencer Cryptowendyo has a vast following on Twitter, Instagram, and TikTok.

What is the number of subscribers on the Crypto WendyO YouTube channel? How much money does she earn from her channel?

WendyO Crypto YouTube Channel @CryptoWendyO (3)[1] has over 1.7K videos and 202k subscribers as of January 24, 2024.

According to Starstat. yt (4)[2], the net worth of CryptoWendyo's Channel is \$102,251 as of 24 January 2024. WendyO earns \$5,440 per month and 65,286 dollars a year

---

1. https://www.youtube.com/@CryptoWendyO

2.   https://starstat.yt/ch/cryptowendyo-net-worth/

What is the formula she shares with her followers for becoming a millionaire?

She gives a successful formula for becoming a millionaire. She emphasizes that risks are often challenging and not always profitable, but you will only succeed with risk.

What do we learn from the life of Crypto WendyO?

We learn from this story that life offers opportunities if you want to change your circumstances. Practical steps need to be taken to take advantage of these opportunities.

The Moral of the Story:

The life of Crypto Wandiyo teaches us that skills or expertise are essential for success in life.

The world has been revolutionized by modern technologies such as blockchain, artificial intelligence, and the metaverse web. It is also possible for you to change your destiny by adopting modern technology.

You may belong to any region of the world, live in any city, village, or town, belong to any age group, or work in any field and are unsuccessful despite being involved for many years. However, your spirit is young, and you are determined to change your circumstances. Because of your dedication, you can change your situation. The circumstances will automatically improve if you take a step forward.

References:

1. Reguerra, E. (2022, May 13). Crypto Stories: YouTuber CryptoWendyO shares how her healthcare skills helped with crypto trading. *Cointelegraph.* https://cointelegraph.com/news/crypto-stories-youtuber-cryptowendyo-shares-how-her-healthcare-skills-helped-with-crypto-trading

2. *Crypto Wendy O Wiki.* (2021c, August 9). https://everipedia.org/wiki/lang_en/wendy-o

3. https://www.youtube.com/@CryptoWendyO

4. StarStat. (2023, November 17). *CryptoWendyO Net Worth, Income & Earnings (2023).* StarStat. https://starstat.yt/ch/cryptowendyo-net-worth/

CRYPTORIES WITH JAVED
THE FIRST COUPLE SPENT THE INITIAL 100 DAYS OF THEIR MARRIED LIFE ON BITCOIN

STORY 08

THE FIRST COUPLE SPENT THE INITIAL 100 DAYS OF THEIR MARRIED LIFE ON BITCOIN

In 2013, an American couple, Austin Craig and Beccy Craig, decided that they would pay all their expenses for the first three months of their marriage or 100 days, including gas, groceries, rent, buying goods, and going on a trip, all of which will be paid with Bitcoin. Later, the documentary (1)[1] "Life on Bitcoin" featured these experiences.

When the couple chose Bitcoin to pay for all their expenses in 2013, it was a very difficult decision.

The reason was that when they asked people in the store, bakery, or gas station, have you heard of Bitcoin? They expressed surprise since they weren't familiar with it.

A bitcoin wallet was required to collect and transfer bitcoins. But people weren't aware of it at all. The couple said that the world has become digital, but digital usage is still limited.

Then there were scenes of The Black Sheep, Utah's finest restaurant, serving 24 bitcoin customers (2)[2] for the first time. It was a fun event where customers enjoyed their favorite foods and drank champagne as well. These users were Utah's early adopters who became part of the Bitcoin community. On the "Life on Bitcoin (3)[3]" YouTube channel, you can watch the video of this first Bitcoin gathering.

In order to accept Bitcoin, the restaurant set up a Bitpay processing system. It processed all the transactions quickly, but it took a long time to clear the last transaction. Bitpay is known for its excellent chain system for restaurant and bar transactions.

---

1. https://tubitv.com/movies/610187/life-on-bitcoin

2.   https://www.youtube.com/watch?v=T_4BVXkS9VM

3.   https://www.youtube.com/@LifeonBitcoin

This documentary is most interesting because it shows people who are interested in Bitcoin coming together and becoming a Bitcoin community, exchanging ideas freely, and learning about a wide variety of products and services.

What was the purpose of making Life on Bitcoin movie?

The purpose of making this film is to promote this incredible technology and make people aware of it. In order to achieve this, they produced a documentary film, for which they raised $70,00 through sponsorships and public donations.

To attain this goal, they made a documentary film, for which they raised 70 thousand dollars through public donations and sponsorships.

When was this documentary made, and when was it aired?

Filming for the documentary began in 2013 and ended in 2017. Notable Media houses, including Hollywood reporters, Fast Company, Bloomberg, and the Wall Street Journal covered the story. You can watch the film on Amazon.

The documentary was filmed in 2013 but completed in 2017. Many prominent Media outlets such as Fast Company, Bloomberg, the Wall Street Journal, and Hollywood reporters covered the story. On Amazon, you can watch this movie.

Over time, the film continued to improve. The original broadcast (4)[1] took place on July 18, 2015, at the Play and Plug Tech Center in Sunnyvale, California. This documentary was made possible by the contributions and sponsorship of many Kickstarter backers.

---

1.   https://news.bitcoin.com/life-bitcoin-producing-film/

The Crux of the story:

The movie **"Life on Bitcoin"** contains expert opinions, talk shows, critics, and commentator's comments.

The media houses raised the question of whether this was a legit use of an unlicensed currency, which is only internet money and can also lead to money laundering, which had been the subject of a scandal like Silk Road, or how it could work. Is it possible to use Bitcoin with fiat currency or dollars? Moreover, it is a very volatile currency, which raises many concerns, including the fear of losing your money.

However, this was also a first step to attracting people to use them in everyday life. The movie urged government regulators to develop a model that regulates the use of cryptocurrencies.

Later on, in view of the increasing popularity of Bitcoin, many countries recognized cryptocurrency, especially Bitcoin, as a legal form of payment. These countries are Estonia, Zug, El Salvador, Switzerland, New Zealand, Japan, and others.

References:

1. Tubi is the largest free movie and TV streaming service in the US. We are not available in Europe due to changes in EU laws. (n.d.). https://tubitv.com/movies/610187/life-on-bitcoin

2. https://www.youtube.com/watch?v=T_4BVXkS9VM

3. https://www.youtube.com/@LifeonBitcoin

4. Redman, J. (2016b, May 10). 'Life On Bitcoin' is Easier Than Producing a Film About it. Bitcoin News. https://news.bitcoin.com/life-bitcoin-producing-film/

MT. GOX HEIST
THE INSIDE STORY OF THE BIGGEST HACK OF 850,000 BITCOINS
8
CRYPTORIES WITH JAVED

STORY 09

MT. GOX HEIST: THE INSIDE STORY OF THE BIGGEST HACK OF 850,000 BITCOINS

What was MT Gox?

In Tokyo, Japan, Mt. G ox was the largest Bitcoin exchange. This exchange handled over 70 percent (1)[1] of Bitcoin transactions between 2010 and 2014.

The Mt. Gox heist, which involved the theft of 850,000 bitcoins, is the grand bitcoin heist in cryptocurrency history. Jed McCaleb founded the Mt. Gox in 2010. Its name is an acronym for Magic: The Gathering Online Exchange (2)[2]. French National Mark Robert Karpeles bought the exchange in 2011. Analysts estimated that 80,000 bitcoins had already vanished before the purchase.

The leading Bitcoin exchange stopped trading activities on February 24, 2014, following the hack of 850,000 bitcoins. The company revealed (3)[3] that it had lost 7500,000 bitcoins of customers and another 100,000 BTC from its holding account. Ultimately, the corporation sought protection from its creditors by filing for bankruptcy in US and Tokyo courts.

Despite being declared bankrupt in 2014, the exchange's legal affairs continued for years. (Bankruptcy protection (4)[4] is a legal process wherein a business owner applies to the court stating that the loss of the business has rendered him or her financially unable to pay the debts; as a result, the owner of the business is permitted to liquidate

1. https://en.wikipedia.org/wiki/Mt._Gox

2.   https://www.investopedia.com/terms/m/
   mt-gox.asp#_853ae90f0351324bd73ea615e6487517__4c761f170e016836ff84498202b99827_
   _853ae90f0351324bd73ea615e6487517_text_43ec3e5dee6e706af7766fffea512721_Key_0bce
   f9c45bd8a48eda1b26eb0c61c869_20Takeaways-_c0cb5f0fcf239ab3d9c1fcd31fff1efc_Mt._c0c
   b5f0fcf239ab3d9c1fcd31fff1efc_operated_0bcef9c45bd8a48eda1b26eb0c61c869_20between_
   0bcef9c45bd8a48eda1b26eb0c61c869_202010_0bcef9c45bd8a48eda1b26eb0c61c869_20and
   _0bcef9c45bd8a48eda1b26eb0c61c869_202014.

3.   https://cointelegraph.com/magazine/crypto-exchange-hacks/

4.   https://www.investopedia.com/terms/b/bankruptcy.asp

the business and give the customers the money that remains after the sale of the assets). A settlement for its restoration in 2021 was agreed by the plaintiffs and the Tokyo District Court around 7.5 years later.

91

What happened to MT. Gox Exchange?

Between 2010 and 2014, the Tokyo-based exchange experienced security issues several times.

In 2011, hackers stole users' information and transferred many bitcoins from their Bitcoin wallets. As a result of a network protocol flaw, the exchange lost thousands of bitcoins in the same year.

On June 19, 2011, hackers took advantage of security flaws, they breached the security (3)[1] and obtained admin-level access to the system. During the attack, hackers created fake bitcoins in bulk quantity, and artificially supplied fake bitcoins through exchange in the market, causing their price to drop dramatically by $0.01 when Bitcoin was trading at $17.50. The hacker withdrew 2000 real bitcoins. Apart from this, they leaked the exchange database, allegedly used the credentials of the users, and hashed passwords.

The company strengthened its security to guard the exchange from these kinds of attacks, but it was powerless to stop them. Mt. Gox disclosed in February 2014, the exchange was compromised in 2011, and hackers stole hundreds of thousands of Bitcoins over a three-year period.

Wired Magazine (5)[2] revealed in November 2013 that customers had to wait weeks to months to withdraw their funds. During the following months, users faced a lot of difficulties withdrawing funds. Technical glitches weakened the company's grip.

Two reasons were mentioned for the delay in obtaining funds from the exchange:

CoinLab sued MT Gox in May 2013 for $75 million for breach of contract, which is one of the main reasons for this. CoinLab signed an agreement with MT Gox North American Services on February 14, 2013, to handle exchange affairs, but MT Gox did not comply with it.

---

1. https://cointelegraph.com/magazine/crypto-exchange-hacks/

2. https://www.wired.com/2013/11/mtgox/

Theft on a large scale is another important reason. As a result of suspicious activity in digital wallets on the exchange, the exchange halted Bitcoin withdrawals in February 2014. A company revealed that 850,000 bitcoins had been lost. Among them were some belonging to the company and others to customers. The lost cryptocurrency destabilized the market.

Later, Mark Karpeles announced (6)[3] that it had found 200,000 bitcoins used in old Bitcoin wallets before June 2011. However, 650,000 bitcoins could not be located. The Bitcoin exchange promised to pay the cash equivalent to the worth of 200,000 bitcoins to the claimants.

The exchange was unable to pay back the millions of dollars in missing bitcoins, so on February 28, 2014, the company filed for bankruptcy in the District Court of Japan. This allowed the defaulters to carry on the company's operation to settle its debts under the restructuring plan. In the meanwhile, several debtors brought lawsuits against the business.

The court issued a dissolution order in April 2014, directing the company's assets to be sold on the free market for cash and given to the claimants. The judiciary froze the funds as a trust.

In August 2015, the company's owner Mark Karpeles was arrested for fraud, embezzlement, and computer system manipulation to inflate company account balances by making false statements. Police suspected that he had misappropriated 341 million Yen (around $3 million) transferred funds from customers' accounts into his account from September to December 2013, and boosted the account balance amount.

On July 14, 2016, Mark was released on bail after paying around $100,000 (7)[4]. The court bound him to stay in Japan and face trial.

---

3.   https://www.mtgox.com/img/pdf/20140320-btc-announce.pdf

4.   https://cointelegraph.com/news/mt-gox-ceo-mark-karpeles-out-on-bail-thinner-than-before

According to Reuters, On July 11, 2017, 32-year-old Mark Karpeles was found not guilty to charges related to the embezzlement of funds. He told to the three Judges of the Tokya Court, Japan, "I swear to God that I am innocent (8)[5]".

Mark Robert Karpeles was not put in jail after the Tokyo District Court sentenced him to 30 months in prison on March 14, 2019, for falsely declaring and inflating the company's assets by $33 million. His sentence was suspended for the following four years. if he did not conduct any more crimes, such as financial theft or breach of trust.

---

5. https://www.reuters.com/article/us-japan-bitcoin-mt-gox-idUSKBN19W07Z

Where did the missing bitcoins go? Who stole it?

The company recovered 200,000 (6)[1] Bitcoins, but not the missing 650,000.

The US Department of Justice (DOJ) charged (9)[2] Russian nationals Alexey Bilyuchenko and Alexander Verner for their involvement in the Bitcoin hacking incident at Mt. Gox on June 09, 2023. Between September 2011 and February 2014, they stole 647,000 BTC (10)[3] from Mt. Gox. They moved the stolen bitcoins to BTC-e, TradeHill, and their personal Mt. Gox accounts. Additionally, different American companies were used to sell the bitcoins.

The U.S. Department of Justice charged the hackers, Bilyuchenko and Verner, of conspiring to launder money. Additionally, Bilyuchenko was accused of running an unregistered money services company. Bilyuchenko and Alexander Vinnik, both (11)[4] were technical operators of BTC-e. Alexander Vinnik was arrested in Greece in 2017. Bilyuchenko was detained in Russia in 2019. BTC-e operator Vinnik has been handed over to the U.S. authorities to face similar charges, after the extradition from Russia and France.

In 2013, the TradeHill exchange closed because of issues with payments and regulations. In 2017, the BTC-e was shut down by US authorities.

---

1. https://www.mtgox.com/img/pdf/20140320-btc-announce.pdf

2. https://www.justice.gov/usao-sdny/pr/russian-nationals-charged-hacking-one-cryptocurrency-exchange-and-illicitly-operating

3. https://www.coindesk.com/policy/2023/06/09/mt-goxs-hackers-are-2-russian-nationals-us-doj-alleges-in-indictment/

4. https://www.coindesk.com/consensus-magazine/2023/06/09/where-the-mt-gox-money-went-new-details-in-the-btc-e-exchange-case/

Bilyuchenko and Alexander Verner could receive a maximum sentence of 20 years in jail if the DOJ finds them guilty of conspiring to commit money laundering.

What is the Mt. Gox Rehabilitation Plan, and how will the Rehabilitation Creditors be paid?

The company was declared bankrupt in 2014, but the litigation dragged on for years without end, and after seven and a half years, on November 16, 2021, creditors and the Rehabilitation trustee of Mt. Gox agreed to the Bitcoin Rehabilitation plan regarding repayment, and this law war ended.

On July 6, 2022, Nobuaki Kobayashi, Attorney-at-law, the court-appointed Rehabilitation trustee for the rehabilitation agreement, issued an official document detailing the repayment procedures under the Rehabilitation plan (12)[1].

According to this plan, Creditors could register their claim for recovery of their funds to Mt. Gox's online claim filing system. The deadline for claim submission was January 10, 2023.

A Tokyo court has limited creditors' claims to recover funds until February 2021. No new claimant could make a fresh claim for recovery of funds under this system.

On April 06, 2023, Mt. Gox announced that the deadline for filing claims for losses had passed. The repayment to all creditors/customers would happen before 31 October 2023. This payment, however, could not be made. On September 21, 2023, the Mt. Gox trustee announced [2]to begin making payments to creditors who had submitted all required information before the end of 2023.

By October 31, 2024, they promised to make the repayment of all the rehabilitation creditors.

---

1.   https://www.mtgox.com/img/pdf/20220706_announcement_en.pdf

2.   https://www.mtgox.com/img/pdf/20230921_announcement_en.pdf

The Crux of the Story:

The majority of hackers prefer to use fraudulent exchanges or exchanges that don't require verification. Exchanges that eliminate KYC procedures and withdrawal limits, making it easy to cash out stolen money. So make sure to choose platforms where KYC and AML practices are meticulously followed. It is preferable to keep your funds in an offline hard wallet instead of an online soft wallet. If it is necessary to keep funds on the platforms, then you must select the option of 2FA verification.

You need to be proactive as a cryptocurrency user to safeguard your investments. Following preventive measures should be taken:

- Use an exchange with robust security protocols, for instance; make strong passwords using a password manager.

- Use Google Authenticator for two-factor authentication instead of Sim-received 2FA.

- Employ a hardware wallet, such as Trezor or Ledger, for large, long-term investments.

- Use software wallets for tiny sums of money.

- Utilize several software wallets for various purposes (trading, lending, etc.).

- Trust Wallet and MetaMask are the preferred options.

- Avoid clicking on any dubious links and shield your devices from infected software by using antivirus software.

● Put your seed phrases or wallet recovery phrases on two to
three pieces of paper and keep them separate.

● Avoid disclosing your passwords or private keys online as
hackers can access them.

Finally, but just as importantly, familiarize yourself with crypto
knowledge. To steer clear of typical blunders, make sure you stay up to
date on crypto forums and networks.

References:

1. Wikipedia contributors. (2023, November 11). Mt. Gox. Wikipedia. https://en.wikipedia.org/wiki/Mt._Gox

2. Frankenfield, J. (2023, May 30). What was Mt. Gox? Definition, history, collapse, and future. Investopedia. https://www.investopedia.com/terms/m/
mt-gox.asp#:~:text=Key%20Takeaways-,Mt.,operated%20between%202010%20an[1].

3. Cointelegraph Magazine.Crypto Hacks: (n.d). Report on Crypto Exchange Hacks 2011-2020. https://cointelegraph.com/magazine/crypto-exchange-hacks/

4. Tuovila, A. (2023, November 22). Bankruptcy Explained: Types and how it works. Investopedia. https://www.investopedia.com/terms/b/bankruptcy.asp

5. McMillan, R., & Metz, C. (2013, November 6). The rise and fall of the world's largest bitcoin exchange. WIRED. https://www.wired.com/2013/11/mtgox/

6. Karpeles. M. (2014, March 20). Notice about the balance of bitcoins (BTC) held by MtGox Co., Ltd. Mt.Gox Co. https://www.mtgox.com/img/pdf/20140320-btc-announce.pdf

7. Campbell, R. (2016, July 14). MT Gox CEO Mark Karpeles out on bail, thinner than before. Cointelegraph. https://cointelegraph.com/news/mt-gox-ceo-mark-karpeles-out-on-bail-thinner-than-before

---

1. https://www.investopedia.com/terms/m/
mt-gox.asp#_853ae90f0351324bd73ea615e6487517__4c761f170e016836ff84498202b99827__853ae90f035132
4bd73ea615e6487517_text_43ec3e5dee6e706af7766fffea512721_Key_0bcef9c45bd8a48eda1b26eb0c61c869_20
Takeaways-_c0cb5f0fcf239ab3d9c1fcd31fff1efc_Mt._c0cb5f0fcf239ab3d9c1fcd31fff1efc_operated_0bcef9c45bd8
a48eda1b26eb0c61c869_20between_0bcef9c45bd8a48eda1b26eb0c61c869_202010_0bcef9c45bd8a48eda1b26e
b0c61c869_20and_0bcef9c45bd8a48eda1b26eb0c61c869_202014

8. Wilson, T. (2017, July 11). Chief of bitcoin exchange Mt. Gox denies embezzlement as trial opens. Reuters. https://www.reuters.com/article/us-japan-bitcoin-mt-gox-idUSKBN19W07Z

9. Leising.M. (2021, jAN.31).'Trillion Dollar' Mt. Gox Demise as Told by a Bitcoin Insider. Bloomberg.com. https://www.bloomberg.com/news/articles/2021-01-31/-trillion-dollar-mt-gox-demise-as-told-by-a-bitcoin-insider

10. The U.S. DOJ. (2023, June 9). Russian nationals charged with hacking one cryptocurrency exchange and illicitly operating another. Press Release. https://www.justice.gov/usao-sdny/pr/russian-nationals-charged-hacking-one-cryptocurrency-exchange-and-illicitly-operating

11. De, N. (2023b, June 9). Mt. Gox's Hackers Are 2 Russian Nationals, U.S. DOJ Alleges in Indictment. Coindesk.https://www.coindesk.com/policy/2023/06/09/mt-goxs-hackers-are-2-russian-nationals-us-doj-alleges-in-indictment/

12. Baydakova, A. (2023, June 13). Where the Mt. Gox Money Went: New Details in the BTC-e Exchange Case. Coindesk.https://www.coindesk.com/consensus-magazine/2023/06/09/where-the-mt-gox-money-went-new-details-in-the-btc-e-exchange-case/

13. Mt.gox Co. (2023, July 6).Information on Repayment Procedures.

https://www.mtgox.com/img/pdf/20220706_announcement_en.pdf

14. Mt.gox Co. (2023, September 21). Notice concerning change of Repayment deadlines.

https://www.mtgox.com/img/pdf/20230921_announcement_en.pdf

CRYPTORIES WITH JAVED
BITCOIN
TREASURE HUNTERS
FIND THE LOST BITCOINS AND
CHANGE THE PEOPLE'S CRYPTO
FORTUNE

STORY 10

BITCOIN TREASURE HUNTERS: FIND LOST BITCOINS AND CHANGE PEOPLE'S CRYPTO FORTUNE

The story (1)[1] is about a father and son living in Illinois, USA, who are called Bitcoin treasure hunters. They help people find their lost cryptocurrency, especially Bitcoin. They helped many people recover lost cryptocurrency worth millions of dollars.

A resident of Illinois named Rhonda Kempert purchased six bitcoins for $80 in 2013. The purchase price of one bitcoin was 13.4 dollars at that time. The next year, she spent two and a half bitcoins but still had 3.5 bitcoins.

This currency was less important in 2013. After a few years, the price of one bitcoin reached 20,000 dollars in 2017, and she remembered her crypto purchase. She was pleased to become the owner of thousands of dollars. She immediately tried to access her Bitcoin wallet to sell her bitcoins, but she had forgotten her wallet login information.

Rhonda Kempert noticed that some of the digits in the wallet's identification digits were missing from the paper she had printed. She had the password but didn't know the wallet ID. She tried for several months and was finally disappointed that she had lost thousands of dollars.

A Bitcoin wallet automatically generates a Bitcoin ID or address when it is created. A BTC wallet ID is a public address for receiving funds. ID is an alphanumeric digit, similar to a bank account number. If you forget the Bitcoin wallet ID, you won't be able to access the Bitcoin stored in the wallet. While the private key is a secret code

---

1. https://www.bbc.com/news/technology-60318946

(password) associated with the wallet ID, it allows you to access and control the funds.

When Bitcoin hit its record high in 2017, it began to fall, even falling below $4000 in March 2020. Then, it suddenly increased to over $50,000 in 2021. Every day, it was growing. This is 600 times more than Rhonda bought eight years ago. The value of her bitcoins had risen to a substantial amount.

She searched the internet for all the possible solutions to recover the lost digital currencies. Meanwhile, she learns about the father-son crypto Treasure hunters who look for lost bitcoins. She immediately contacted them. After talking for a while, Rhonda gave them all the information they needed when she gained their trust. The woman joined them on a video call and watched what happened. Eventually, crypto hunters were able to open the Bitcoin wallet. She was overjoyed when she saw 3.5 bitcoins in her wallet after eight years, worth $175,000.

She paid Chris 20% of the promised amount and spent $10,000 of the remaining amount on her daughter's college tuition.

She stored all her wallet information on a hard drive when she accessed her Bitcoins. It is similar to a USB drive but not connected to the internet so that you can store confidential information offline. Rhonda Kempert kept the bitcoins for her retirement plan.

Who are Treasure Hunters, and how did their popularity grow?

An American father and son are treasure hunters from Illinois. Fifty-year-old Chris is a computer engineer who founded the Crypto Asset Recovery company in 2017 but soon got involved with another project. In 2020, when Charlie, his 20-year-old son, returned home from college vacation, the father and son decided to restart Crypto Asset Recovery. In Hampshire, they started working from home.

As a result of their skill in work, father and son quickly became popular. Their job is to assist users in obtaining their tokens by providing access to non-custodial wallet secret keys and wallet login passwords. Non-custodial wallets are called self-custody wallets. The users have complete control over their funds, and they own their private keys. On the other hand, Custodial wallets are controlled by a third party, and they take custody of the private key instead of the wallet owner.

According to a survey by CryptoVantage (2)[1] in 2021, 39.7 percent of cryptocurrency owners forget their passwords, of which 95.6 people say that they have regained access to their investments, while 11.9 percent of respondents believe that their wallet passwords are unsafe.

Chainalysis reports that 18.6 million bitcoins have been mined, of which 20%, i.e., 3.7 million, are missing. The value of which is in billions of dollars. One of the main causes is the loss of wallet login passwords or private keys.

Treasure hunters have many chances of success in this field. In 2020, Bitcoin's price began to rise in the second quarter until November 2021, when it reached an extreme level of $67,000. Many users contacted them during this time, and they recovered many people's digital currencies.

---

1.   https://www.cryptovantage.com/cryptocurrency-storage-security/

Charlie had to give up his computer science degree as their business grew. On days when the price of bitcoin was rising, he received about 100 emails and calls daily.

In 2021, they returned over a million dollars worth of bitcoins to their users.

How do treasure hunters recover passwords?

The treasure hunter asks many questions of the asset owner. In their view, people use passwords that are related to them in their personal lives or code words that they have used a lot in the past, like their date of birth, childhood friend, or pet's name. It can also be the last password entered on Google.

When they obtain the password, they get 20% of the entire wallet currency as a reward for their efforts.

What problems might they encounter?

For their work, they have to travel to other countries besides America. They sometimes have to deal with many problems at work. Time, effort, and money are wasted when the wallet is inaccessible. For example, In 2021, treasure hunters experienced an unpleasant incident (3)[1]. In Savannah, Georgia, one of his clients claimed to have 5,000 thousand bitcoins in his wallet after winning a court case. At that time, it was worth 44 million dollars. Charlie said that when he spoke with him on the phone, the client said we could withdraw up to $300,000 weekly, but we wanted to withdraw everything. In addition, he promised to make them millionaires.

The following day, they were picked up by three tall men at the airport when they arrived in Georgia.

The father and son were nervous as they attempted to pressure them. A claim for $44 million had increased to $3.2 billion, and it was not in Bitcoin but Ethereum. Using their laptops, both experts managed to combine seed phrases. When they opened the wallet, they found $10 only.

In many such cases, they have to rely on the information given by the client, even if that information is wrong.

---

1. https://www.thenationalnews.com/business/money/2022/03/25/bitcoin-treasure-hunters-the-father-and-son-team-who-recover-lost-cryptocurrencies/

The Crux of the story:

There are many examples in the crypto world where you have lost thousands of bitcoins forever just because you forgot your password or you lost the device where you saved your password.

Any user needs to understand the usage and the importance of wallet ID, seed phrases, and private keys to secure and access their capital.

A wallet ID is a specific, private identifier for your Bitcoin wallet. It verifies your identity and cryptocurrency wallet ownership. This is like a password; through this, you log in to your wallet. If it is lost, you cannot log into your wallet or manage your funds.

Seed phrases consist of 12-24 randomly generated secret words that you use to gain access to one or more wallets on the blockchain. It helps to recover lost wallets. Seed phrases are also called recovery phrases. In contrast, a private key gives access to a wallet address. That is, it connects you to your account from which you can withdraw or transfer funds.

You should write your Bitcoin wallet information on paper and keep it with your documents at two or three locations. Keep your assets safe with an offline hard drive like the Ledger Nano X or Trezor Model T.

References:

1. Tidy, J. (2022, February 10). 'Hackers helped me find my lost Bitcoin fortune.' *BBC News*. https://www.bbc.com/news/technology-60318946

2. *Coin Storage Security*. (n.d.). https://www.cryptovantage.com/cryptocurrency-storage-security/

3. Glover, F. (2022, March 25). Bitcoin treasure hunters: the father-and-son team who recover lost cryptocurrencies. *The National*. https://www.thenationalnews.com/business/money/2022/03/25/bitcoin-treasure-hunters-the-father-and-son-team-who-recover-lost-cryptocurrencies/

CRYPTORIES WITH JAVED
CELEBRITY
Kim Kardashian
WAS FINED $1.26 MILLION FOR PROMOTING CRYPTOCURRENCY ON INSTAGRAM

STORY 11

CELEBRITY KIM KARDASHIAN WAS FINED $1.26 MILLION FOR PROMOTING CRYPTOCURRENCY ON INSTAGRAM

A celebrity was fined $1.26 (1)[1] million for advertising cryptocurrency on social media. Kim Kardashian is a celebrity. She gets millions of dollars by advertising different brands.

The Security Exchange Commission (SEC) fined (2)[2] reality TV star Kardashian $1.26 million on October 3, 2022. In her Instagram post, she was accused of illegally promoting the new cryptocurrency Ethereum Max. She took two and a half million dollars to publish the post. However, this amount was not disclosed, violating the Federal Securities Act law of SEC's securities.

Her failure to disclose this amount contravenes the Federal Securities Act law of SEC's securities.

Kim asked people on her Instagram (3)[3] on June 13, 2021, "Are you guys into crypto?". She then explained that what I am sharing with you

---

1. https://www.forbes.com/sites/siladityaray/2022/10/03/kim-kardashian-agrees-to-pay-126-million-to-settle-sec-cryptocurrency-promotion-suit/?sh=1719b6a448b6

2. https://www.sec.gov/news/press-release/2022-183#_853ae90f0351324bd73ea615e6487517__4c761f170e016836ff84498202b99827__853ae90f0351324bd73ea615e6487517_text_43ec3e5dee6e706af7766fffea512721_The_0bcef9c45bd8a48eda1b26eb0c61c869_20Securities_0bcef9c45bd8a48eda1b26eb0c61c869_20and_0bcef9c45bd8a48eda1b26eb0c61c869_20Exchange_0bcef9c45bd8a48eda1b26eb0c61c869_20Commission_c0cb5f0fcf239ab3d9c1fcd31fff1efc_she_0bcef9c45bd8a48eda1b26eb0c61c869_20received_0bcef9c45bd8a48eda1b26eb0c61c869_20for_0bcef9c45bd8a48eda1b26eb0c61c869_20the_0bcef9c45bd8a48eda1b26eb0c61c869_20promotion

3. https://www.cnbc.com/2021/06/15/kim-kardashian-west-charli-damelio-jake-paul-posting-paid-crypto-ads.html

is what my friends told me about the Ethereum Max token. In this post, she urged her 330 million followers to invest in tokens.

Kim also included some hashtags in this post, including the company hashtag and #ad hashtag.

Kim had another charge for promoting a pump-and-dump scheme. In a pump and dump scheme, the buyer is pumped, i.e., the price of the coin is artificially inflated by misleading the buyer and then sold to uninformed customers at a higher price, i.e., dump.

How much did the SEC fine Kim for declaring this post illegal?

Kardashian violated the anti-touting provision of the federal securities laws. Consequently, she was charged $250,000 of disgorgement and $10,000 of profits totaling $260,000 by SEC. Additionally, a one million dollar fine was imposed. Thus, Kim was fined $1.26 million, which Kim agreed to pay. Kim promised to refrain from promoting any cryptocurrency for the next three years.

SEC Chairman Gary Gensler explained how promoting crypto assets differs from promoting other products and services.

In one of his tweets (4)[1], he said celebrity skills should not be confused with the skills necessary to give sound investment advice.

Additionally, many celebrity market products, such as clothes, perfumes, and cosmetics, need skills that differ from investment skills. Therefore, they should not be advised to invest in cryptocurrencies. It is an area in which celebrities are neither familiar nor skilled.

Celebrities and influencers who endorse investments, including crypto-asset securities, may not be suited to everyone.

---

1.   https://twitter.com/GaryGensler/status/1576897535427448832

What made Ethereum Max Token famous?

The project introduced itself as a cultural token that its users could use at concerts or sporting events.

Tickets can also be purchased using Ethereum Max. In one example, Tokens were used to pay for tickets to see Floyd Mayweather fight Vs Logan Paul. However, no major cryptocurrency exchange listed the currency, and it was not linked to Ethereum in any way.

The token was popularised by celebrities who promoted the pump and dump scheme to promote the token.

As a result, Ethereum Max had lost 97% (5)[1] of its value by June 2022. Several investors have lost money by investing in Ethereum Max.

In response to this illegal advertisement, Kim and other celebrities were sued. Floyd Mayweather is one of them.

---

1. https://www.theverge.com/2022/10/3/23384789/kim-kardashian-crypto-fine-sec-pump-and-dump-ethereum-max

What was the impact of Kim's fine on her income?

Kim has a personal net worth of $1.8 billion at that time, currently it stands on $1.7 billion (6)[1] as of January 07, 2024. It is not a big deal for Kim to pay this fine, but it will teach her and many other celebrities to respect US Asset Securities Laws in the future.

1. https://www.forbes.com/profile/kim-kardashian/?sh=369b397c5230

The Crux of the Story:

By targeting Kim, the SEC sent a message to other influencers that anyone promoting cryptocurrency or any other investment must comply with securities laws.

Additionally, celebrities don't give their followers any investment advice that could risk their money because this is not the area of stars. Encouraging investment in this field requires special skills that celebrities don't have.

References:

1. Ray, S. (2022, October 3). Kim Kardashian Agrees To Pay $1.26 Million To Settle SEC Cryptocurrency Promotion Charge. Forbes. https://www.forbes.com/sites/siladityaray/2022/10/03/kim-kardashian-agrees-to-pay-126-million-to-settle-sec-cryptocurrency-promotion-suit/?sh=550036c348b6

2. SEC.gov | SEC Charges Kim Kardashian for Unlawfully Touting Crypto Security. (2022, October 3). https://www.sec.gov/news/press-release/2022-183#:~:text=The%20Securities%20and%20Exchange%20Commission,[1]

3. Locke, T. (2021, June 22). Kim Kardashian West and other influencers are being paid to advertise cryptocurrency on social media. CNBC. https://www.cnbc.com/2021/06/15/kim-kardashian-west-charli-damelio-jake-paul-posting-paid-crypto-ads.html

4. https://twitter.com/GaryGensler/status/1576897535427448832

5. Vincent, J. (2022, October 3). Kim Kardashian pays $1.26 million after being charged with illegally promoting crypto scheme. The Verge. https://www.theverge.com/2022/10/3/23384789/kim-kardashian-crypto-fine-sec-pump-and-dump-ethereum-max

6. Kim Kardashian. (n.d.). Forbes. https://www.forbes.com/profile/kim-kardashian/?sh=607cad595230

---

[1]. https://www.sec.gov/news/press-release/2022-183#_853ae90f0351324bd73ea615e6487517__4c761f170e016836ff84498202b99827__853ae90f0351324bd73ea615e6487517_text_43ec3e5dee6e706af7766fffea512721_The_0bcef9c45bd8a48eda1b26eb0c61c869_20Securities_0bcef9c45bd8a48eda1b26eb0c61c869_20and_0bcef9c45bd8a48eda1b26eb0c61c869_20Exchange_0bcef9c45bd8a48eda1b26eb0c61c869_20Commission_c0cb5f0fcf239ab3d9c1fcd31fff1efc_she_0bcef9c45bd8a48eda1b26eb0c61c869_20received_0bcef9c45bd8a48eda1b26eb0c61c869_20for_0bcef9c45bd8a48eda1b26eb0c61c869_20the_0bcef9c45bd8a48eda1b26eb0c61c869_20promotion

ON THE DARK WEB
JAMES ZHONG
STOLE 51,000 BITCOINS
WORTH OVER 3.4 BILLION DOLLARS.
HOW DID HE DO IT?
CRYPTORIES
WITH
JAVED

STORY 12

JAMES ZHONG STOLE 51,000 BITCOINS WORTH OVER 3.4 BILLION DOLLARS ON THE DARK WEB. HOW DID HE DO IT?

Financial Times, Fortune, CNBC, Guardian, Forbes, Cointelegraph, and the BBC, among other world's leading newspapers, published a shocking story on November 7, 2022, in which the U.S. Department of Justice claimed (1)[1] that it had seized the second-largest bitcoin heist and recovered 51,680 bitcoins valued $3.4 billion stolen in 2012.

James Zhong committed Bitcoin theft on the notorious dark website known as Silk Road.

Silk Road (2)[2] was an online black market where drugs, money laundering, services, and products were bought and sold through cryptocurrency. The marketplace was used for illicit activities from 2011 to 2013. It is also known as the Amazon of drugs. Ross William Ulbricht founded the dark web. The FBI arrested him in 2013 and convicted him of seven Silk Road-related charges in 2015. Consequently, he was imprisoned for life in 2015.

---

1. https://www.justice.gov/usao-sdny/pr/silk-road-dark-web-fraud-defendant-sentenced-following-seizure-and-forfeiture-over-

   34#_853ae90f0351324bd73ea615e6487517__4c761f170e016836ff84498202b99827__853ae90f0351324bd73ea615e6487517_text_43ec3e5dee6e706af7766fffea512721_Damian_0bcef9c45bd8a48eda1b26eb0c61c869_20Williams_0bcef9c45bd8a48eda1b26eb0c61c869_2C_0bcef9c45bd8a48eda1b26eb0c61c869_20the_0bcef9c45bd8a48eda1b26eb0c61c869_20United_0bcef9c45bd8a48eda1b26eb0c61c869_20States_c0cb5f0fcf239ab3d9c1fcd31fff1efc_Road_0bcef9c45bd8a48eda1b26eb0c61c869_20dark_0bcef9c45bd8a48eda1b26eb0c61c869_20web_0bcef9c45bd8a48eda1b26eb0c61c869_20internet_0bcef9c45bd8a48eda1b26eb0c61c869_20marketplace.

2. https://en.wikipedia.org/wiki/Silk_Road_(marketplace)

How did James steal the bitcoins?

Taking advantage of a flaw in the dark web's payment system, James stole many bitcoins. Taylor Hatcher, an IRS agent, said Zhong created nine accounts. He kept their addresses secret and kept his identity hidden. Each account held 200 to 2000 bitcoins. When he withdrew Bitcoin from his account, he withdrew many coins at once using a technique. He fraudulently transferred over 50,000 bitcoins to these nine accounts through 140 transactions (3)[1].

James' house in Gainesville, Georgia, was searched on November 9, 2019, by U.S. authorities who found hidden Bitcoin private keys in hard drives, underground floor cupboards, and small computers in tin cans taken from washroom cabinets. At that time, it was valued at $3.36 billion. Even though Bitcoin's value has decreased slightly, they are still worth over a billion dollars. Additionally, six hundred sixty thousand dollars in cash were recovered from the hacker.

---

1. https://fortune.com/2022/11/08/justice-department-seizes-50000-bitcoin-silk-road-popcorn-tin/amp/

What arguments did James's lawyer make in his defense?

James' lawyer, Michael Bechner, defended him in court by saying he had been in prison for two years and was deeply remorseful for the crime he committed ten years ago. His age at the time was 22 (4)[1].

Furthermore, his lawyer said that his client had returned all the bitcoins related to the transactions for which he was convicted. It's worth much more now than when it was acquired.

Additionally, his client agreed to liquidate his stake in JZ Capital LLC and gave up $661,900 in cash and other assets.

For so many years, the accused hid his crime. The American authorities confiscated bitcoins from the suspect after the theft was caught. So James was convicted of wire fraud.

---

1. https://www.theguardian.com/technology/2022/nov/07/us-justice-department-seizes-bitcoin-theft

What punishment did Zong receive in this trial?

On February 4, 2020, Zong pleaded guilty before U.S. District Judge Paul Gardephe. On April 14, 2023, the United States Department of Justice sentenced (5)[1] Zhong to one year and one day in prison for wire fraud committed in September 2012 when he illegally siphoned (6)[2] over 50,000 bitcoins from the Silk Road Dark Web.

---

1. https://cointelegraph.com/news/individual-behind-3-4b-silk-road-bitcoin-theft-sentenced-to-one-year-in-prison

2. https://www.cnbc.com/2022/11/07/feds-seize-3point36-billion-in-bitcoin-the-second-largest-recovery-so-far.html

Has cryptocurrency been stolen like this in the past?

Cryptocurrencies have been stolen many times from different exchanges (6)[1] due to flaws in the payment processing system.

M.T. Gox (7)[2] exchange had 850,000 bitcoins stolen in 2014, making it the world's largest bitcoin theft. Zhong's BTC heist is the second significant theft in which many bitcoins have been seized.

The Bitfinix exchange was hacked in 2016, and digital currency worth $3.6 billion was confiscated in 2021.

Through a smart contract coding error, a hacker from Binance, the world's largest crypto exchange, hacked the exchange's native currency, BNB tokens, worth $570 million in October 2022.

In March 2022, a hacker exploited a vulnerability in the Ronin Network decentralized platform and stole $600 million worth of currency.

In July 2022, Chainalysis (8)[3] reported that $1.9 billion worth of crypto was stolen from its platform.

---

1. https://www.cnbc.com/2022/11/07/feds-seize-3point36-billion-in-bitcoin-the-second-largest-recovery-so-far.html

2. https://en.wikipedia.org/wiki/Mt._Gox

3. https://www.chainalysis.com/blog/crypto-crime-midyear-update-2022/?fbclid=IwAR2RiZCukX6FUwkHRH11N_LzDtCfwtnYxKNNvYqWRBlxuuCdRk3SX zthu5c

The Moral of the Story:

We should take all possible steps to secure our crypto assets from hackers, such as using cold wallets (or hardware wallets such as Electrum and Ledger Nano X) that do not connect to the internet. Consequently, they are less susceptible to hacking; you should always use a secure internet connection when making cryptocurrency transactions. If you use public Wi-Fi or unsecured internet, hackers can access your crypto wallet; Storing your cryptocurrency in multiple wallets is possible. Then, even if one wallet is compromised, the others will be safe, and Seed phrases are used to recover your wallet if you lose it. Ensure that they are stored safely and securely.

References:

1. Silk Road Dark Web Fraud Defendant Sentenced Following Seizure And Forfeiture Of Over \$3.4 Billion In Cryptocurrency. (2023, April 14). https://www.justice.gov/usao-sdny/pr/silk-road-dark-web-fraud-defendant-sentenced-following-seizure-and-forfeiture-over-34#:~:text=Damian%20Williams%2C%20the%20United%20States,Road%20dar [1]

2. Wikipedia contributors. Silk Road (marketplace). Wikipedia. https://en.wikipedia.org/wiki/Silk_Road_(marketplace)

3. Morris, C. (2022, November 08). Feds say they seized 50,000 stolen Bitcoin stored in a popcorn tin after a 10-year search. Fortune.com. https://fortune.com/2022/11/08/justice-department-seizes-50000-bitcoin-silk-road-popcorn-tin/amp/

4. The Guardian. (2022, November 7). US justice department seizes bitcoins worth more than \$3bn stolen a decade ago. The Guardian. https://www.theguardian.com/technology/2022/nov/07/us-justice-department-seizes-bitcoin-theft

5. Wright, T. (2023, April 14). Individual behind \$3.4B Silk Road Bitcoin theft sentenced to one year in prison. Cointelegraph. https://cointelegraph.com/news/individual-behind-3-4b-silk-road-bitcoin-theft-sentenced-to-one-year-in-prison

6. Tortorelli, P. (2022, November 21). Feds announce seizure of \$3.36 billion

---

1. https://www.justice.gov/usao-sdny/pr/silk-road-dark-web-fraud-defendant-sentenced-following-seizure-and-forfeiture-over-34#_853ae90f0351324bd73ea615e6487517__4c761f170e016836ff84498202b99827__853ae90f0351324bd73ea615e6487517_text_43ec3e5dee6e706af7766fffea512721_Damian_0bcef9c45bd8a48eda1b26eb0c61c869_20Williams_0bcef9c45bd8a48eda1b26eb0c61c869_2C_0bcef9c45bd8a48eda1b26eb0c61c869_20the_0bcef9c45bd8a48eda1b26eb0c61c869_20United_0bcef9c45bd8a48eda1b26eb0c61c869_20States_c0cb5f0fcf239ab3d9c1fcd31fff1efc_Road_0bcef9c45bd8a48eda1b26eb0c61c869_20dark_0bcef9c45bd8a48eda1b26eb0c61c869_20web_0bcef9c45bd8a48eda1b26eb0c61c869_20internet_0bcef9c45bd8a48eda1b26eb0c61c869_20marketplace

in bitcoin stolen a decade ago from illegal Silk Road marketplace—the second-largest crypto recovery. CNBC. https://www.cnbc.com/2022/11/07/feds-seize-3point36-billion-in-bitcoin-the-second-largest-recovery-so-far.html

7. Wikipedia contributors. (2023b, December 27). *Mt. Gox*. Wikipedia. https://en.wikipedia.org/wiki/Mt._Gox

8. Jardine, E. (2022, August 16). Mid-year crypto crime Update: Illicit activity falls with rest of market, with some notable exceptions. Chainalysis. https://www.chainalysis.com/blog/crypto-crime-midyear-update-2022/?fbclid=IwAR2RiZCukX6FUwkHRH11N_LzDtCfwtnYxKNNvYqW

CRYPTORIES WITH JAVED
DUO KWON'S
TERRA LUNA TRAGEDY
THE LURE OF HIGH PROFITS LOST $42 BILLION OF CRYPTO INVESTORS

STORY 13

DUO KWON'S TERRA LUNA TRAGEDY: THE LURE OF HIGH PROFITS LOST 40 BILLION DOLLARS OF CRYPTO INVESTORS.

This is the story of Duo Kwon's Terra Luna crash. In May 2022, Do Kwon's Terra and Luna currencies collapsed until the value of both reached near zero, which caused investors to lose around 40 billion dollars (1)[1]. In South Korea, 280,000 people lost their capital, and the entire cryptocurrency market lost over 500 billion dollars (2)[2].

Crypto Boss Kwon is charged with having an alleged role in committing fraud and manipulating the market.

Investors sold both currencies in a frenzy, resulting in a collapse of the system. These currencies were among the top ten cryptocurrencies and the world's most popular currencies.

It was the world's most giant crash in crypto history. Most people lost their life savings. This negatively affected currencies such as Bitcoin, Ethereum, etc.

Cryptocurrency king Duo Kwon and his company Terra Labs are facing serious charges (3)[3] of fraud involving billions of dollars in crypto-securities assets, misrepresentation, fraudulently obtaining money from investors, and violating capital market laws.

---

1. https://cointelegraph.com/news/do-kwon-reportedly-arrested-in-montenegro

2. https://www.brecorder.com/news/40198181/wanted-crypto-founder-do-kwon-says-not-on-the-run

3. https://cointelegraph.com/news/sec-sues-do-kwon-and-terraform-labs-for-fraud

What caused the crash of TerraUSD and Luna?

Duo Kwon introduced TerraUSD as a stablecoin. Stablecoins are pegged to real currencies, such as dollars, pounds, euros, etc. The value of Terra is tied to the dollar's value, making it more stable than cryptocurrencies. However, the reality was quite different.

In this case, the stability of the Terra USD (an algorithm stablecoin) was linked to its sister cryptocurrency, LUNA, instead of a dollar.

Duo Kwon had an idea that if the value of TerraUSD falls below one dollar (4)[1], the user could swap it for Luna worth one dollar and earn a profit. Similarly, if the value of TerraUSD rises above one dollar, the user could still swap it for Luna worth one dollar and make a profit. This worked well for some time and kept TerraUSD at one dollar.

But this mechanism only worked for a long time if people wanted Luna. The price of TerraUSD plunged to pennies in May 2022, while Luna fell by more than 99 percent from its peak of $116 [2]to $0.0001 (5)[3], losing around $40 billion of investors in Terra Luna collapse. People's panic selling (6)[4] further worsened the situation.

Another main reason for Terra's crash is that Duo Kwon marketed TerraUST as a stablecoin and promised investors annual returns of up to twenty percent. The promise of huge profits enticed people. This practice goes against the crypto market's principles.

---

1.   https://www.cnbc.com/2022/05/11/terra-ust-stablecoin-dives-below-1-peg-luna-cryptocurrency-down-80percent.html

2.   https://milkroad.com/crashes/

3.   https://milkroad.com/crashes/

4.   https://www.theverge.com/2022/5/20/23131647/terra-luna-do-kwon-stablecoin-anchor

How did the Anchor protocol sink Terra?

Anchor protocol is also called Defi protocol. It is an invention of Terraform Labs that created Terra and Luna.

Terra Labs assured investors that they would receive twenty percent (6)[1] annual profit using Anchor protocol, a phenomenal return compared to the world's number one cryptocurrency exchange, Binance. Binance offers ten percent annual returns on BUSD savings accounts.

Investors believed they could get less return on government bonds and bank savings accounts than the scheme offered. This scheme appealed to them. Under the Anchor Lending Program, you deposit 10,000 Terra, and your deposits are lent to other investors. Other investors must make some Terra deposits as collateral to secure the loan. A certain amount of the interest from this collateral is given to the depositor of the earlier collateral, and the borrower is also rewarded with about 7% annual interest as a reward.

Unlike other stablecoins such as Tether or USDC, Terra didn't directly connect to a reserve but acted as an algorithmic stablecoin that tried to connect to a dollar through an arbitrage process (Difference in prices between both) with its sister token, Luna. When many investors made massive withdrawals, this algorithmic stablecoin failed to stabilize at one dollar.

According to some, it was a Ponzi scheme where the money received by later investors was paid to earlier investors as profit.

---

1.   https://www.theverge.com/2022/5/20/23131647/terra-luna-do-kwon-stablecoin-anchor

Kwon promoted Terra in what way?

Kwon spent $38.5 million (7)[1] on advertising to promote Terra Ecosystem. He also lured countless retail investors to invest from his Twitter account. The top three enterprises (6)[2], Arrows Capital, Jump Crypto, and Pantera Capital, supported Transform Labs. He named Luna Stablecoin after his daughter Luna.

---

1. https://www.coindesk.com/business/2022/05/15/at-nationals-ballpark-terras-bad-week-never-happened/

2. https://www.theverge.com/2022/5/20/23131647/terra-luna-do-kwon-stablecoin-anchor

What legal action has the South Korean government taken against Duo Kwon?

According to a Bloomberg (8)[1] report on September 26, 2022, at the request of South Korean authorities, Interpol published a red notice to apprehend the crypto boss of the controversial and collapsed Terraform Labs ecosystem, accused of losing people's capital of $40 billion in cryptocurrency. The red notice (9)[2] means that law enforcement agencies worldwide will assist the South Korean government in finding and arresting the suspect. The prosecutors in South Korea had already issued a warrant for his arrest on September 14, 2022. He was accused of fraud charges and violation of market laws.

The Singapore Police reported that Duo had been missing since the end of April. On September 17, 2022, he tweeted (2)[3] that he had not absconded and would fully cooperate with government agencies.

Kwon allegedly violated capital market laws. The project's owner denied allegations that the project was a fraud. He said that he had not committed fraud; his own money had been lost in Terra's Crash as well.

He faces numerous legal challenges in different jurisdictions. Over 350 international investors have filed a $57 million lawsuit (10)[4] against him in a Singapore court.

They claimed that they had lost $57 million due to the collapse of TerraUSD's algorithm, a stablecoin. Terraform Labs' spokesperson denied these allegations. He described this as a public market event.

---

1. https://www.bloomberg.com/news/articles/2022-09-26/south-korea-says-interpol-issued-red-notice-for-terra-s-do-kwon?leadSource=uverify%20wall

2. https://www.interpol.int/en/How-we-work/Notices/Red-Notices/View-Red-Notices

3. https://www.brecorder.com/news/40198181/wanted-crypto-founder-do-kwon-says-not-on-the-run

4. https://www.wsj.com/livecoverage/stock-market-news-today-10-28-2022/card/do-kwon-s-other-legal-headache-a-57-million-fraud-lawsuit-in-singapore-5Ix58bBezltt5E95tTI2

Furthermore, he stated that we had disclosed the project's risks to the public.

Eventually, Transform Labs was sued on September 23, 2022. It is alleged that they misrepresented TerraUST, a stablecoin, despite knowing its structural flaws. They persuaded investors to buy digital assets by making false statements.

When and how was Du Kwon arrested?

South Korean Cryptocurrency Boss Du Kwon was arrested (1)[1] at Podgorica (Montenegro) airport on 23 March 2023 with his partner, former Blockchain Aide Executive Han Chang Joon. Joon and Kwon used forged documents to fly from Costa Rica to Dubai. Traveling with forged documents can result in a three-year prison sentence. Filip Adzic, Minister of Interior of Montenegro, confirmed Du Kwon's arrest in his tweet (11)[2]. Regulatory Authorities in Singapore, South Korea, and the United States were searching for the Duo.

The disgraced crypto executive has been detained since March 2023 and is in prison in Podgorica, Montenegro.

In the US and South Korea, authorities are pursuing multiple charges against the notorious crypto executive. He will face these cases and get the punishment when the time comes.

South Korea's local newspaper Vijesti (12)[3] reported that Filip Adzic (13)[4], Minister of Interior of Montenegro, confirmed Dokwon's arrest in his tweet on March 23, 2023. South Korea, Singapore, and US regulatory authorities wanted him.

---

1. https://cointelegraph.com/news/do-kwon-reportedly-arrested-in-montenegro

2. https://twitter.com/filip_adzic/status/1638886164118802432

3. https://www.vijesti.me/vijesti/crna-hronika/649046/jedan-od-najtrazenijih-bjegunaca-i-jos-jedan-drzavljanin-juzne-koreje-uhapseni-u-crnoj-gori-upotrijebili-lazne-isprave

4. https://cointelegraph.com/news/do-kwon-faces-fraud-charges-from-us-prosecutors-hours-after-arrest

What charges did the United States charge against him?

A few hours after Terraform Labs CEO Du Kwon's arrest on March 23, 2023, he was indicted on eight (13)[1] different charges, including securities fraud, commodities fraud, wire fraud, conspiracy to commit fraud, and market manipulation.

In particular, Four charges related to misleading statements made about the TerraUSD stablecoin to maintain its link with the USD and allegedly designing the trading strategies to manipulate (14)[2] the market price of TerraUSD.

The Securities and Exchange Commission (SEC) (15)[3] filed fraud charges against Terraform Labs and Duo Kwon on February 16, 2023, about the loss of $40 billion Terra Luna Classic and algorithmic stablecoin, Terra Classic USD.

---

1. https://cointelegraph.com/news/do-kwon-faces-fraud-charges-from-us-prosecutors-hours-after-arrest

2. https://news.bitcoin.com/report-south-korean-prosecutors-accuse-do-kwon-of-manipulating-lunas-market-price/

3. https://www.sec.gov/news/press-release/2023-32

Is this considered the biggest fraud in crypto history?

Yes, it is considered one of the biggest frauds in crypto history, in which people lost 40 to 50 billion dollars. The crypto market crashed, and crypto users lost 500 billion dollars (2) [1]globally. Earlier in 2017, Dr. Ruja Ignatova cheated more than three million people and disappeared with more than four billion dollars. Duo Kwon's fraud in the crypto market caused 100 times more losses than Roja's.

---

1. https://www.brecorder.com/news/40198181/wanted-crypto-founder-do-kwon-says-not-on-the-run

How did Crypto Queen Ruja Ignatova and Crypto King Duo Kwon scam people?

Bulgarian cryptoQueen Ruja Ignatova exaggeratedly promoted the fake cryptocurrency OneCoin. She predicted that OneCoin would change people's destinies and surpass Bitcoin one day. However, OneCoin was not a cryptocurrency; it was not built on any blockchain.

Similarly, Duo Kwon persuaded investors to invest in the TerraUST by luring them with large profits and declaring it a stablecoin whose value is linked to the dollar. However, TerraUST was not linked to the dollar but to its sister cryptocurrency, LUNA. As a result of TERRA's crash, LUNA also crashed.

What was the reaction of people after the Terra Luna crash?

Terra Luna's crash traumatized many people. The investors lost their lifetime earnings. On the Reddit online community website, people shared suicide prevention tips so that people wouldn't commit suicide due to financial loss shock.

Does Crypto Need to be Regularized?

A crypto regulatory system exists. However, its rules and regulations should be strengthened and enforced.

Cryptocurrency relies on a decentralized blockchain and can't be converted into a centralized one. The crypto community supports this system. Financial institutions and governments cannot control crypto, so a system is necessary to prevent fraud. Educating people about cryptocurrencies is essential to avoid fraud so they know which currency is worth investing in and which is not.

The Moral of the Story:

Cryptocurrency owners who cheat often exaggerate the value of their coins. The lure of high returns attracts investors to digital assets. Many small investors invest in such cryptocurrencies when they see that big investors are investing in them, increasing the demand for coins or stablecoins. Extensive media advertisements draw people's attention to the currency, and they invest their lifetime savings into it.

Do Kwon was not the only one to scam people by promising huge profits; the crypto queen Ruja Ignatova, Sam Bankman Freud, and two African brothers also committed fraud by luring them with high gains.

Therefore, don't get tempted to invest in extensively advertised currencies. Learn all you can about a currency before making a decision.

The rules and regulations must be strengthened, and their enforcement should be ensured. An educated community is essential for the stability of the cryptocurrency system.

References:

1. Sun, Z. (2023, March 23). Breaking: Terraform Labs co-founder Do Kwon reportedly arrested in Montenegro. *Cointelegraph.* https://cointelegraph.com/news/do-kwon-reportedly-arrested-in-montenegro

2. Afp. (2022, September 18). Wanted crypto founder Do Kwon says 'not on the run' *Brecorder.*https://www.brecorder.com/news/40198181/wanted-crypto-founder-do-kwon-says-not-on-the-run

3. Coghlan, J. (2023, February 16). Breaking: SEC sues Do Kwon and Terraform Labs for fraud. *Cointelegraph.* https://cointelegraph.com/news/sec-sues-do-kwon-and-terraform-labs-for-fraud

4. Browne, R. (2022, May 11). Controversial stablecoin UST — which is meant to be pegged to the dollar — plummets below 30 cents. *CNBC.* https://www.cnbc.com/2022/05/11/terra-ust-stablecoin-dives-below-1-peg-luna-cryptocurrency-down-80percent.html

5. Milk Road. (2023, July 6). *A History Of Crypto Crashes.* https://milkroad.com/crashes/

6. Lopatto, E. (2022, May 20). How the Anchor protocol helped sink Terra. *The Verge.* https://www.theverge.com/2022/5/20/23131647/terra-luna-do-kwon-stablecoin-anchor

7. Tan, E., Nelson, D., & Seward, Z. (2023, May 11). At Nationals Ballpark, Terra's Bad Week Never Happened. *Coindesk.com.* https://www.coindesk.com/business/2022/05/15/at-nationals-ballpark-terras-bad-week-never-happened/

8. Cha, S. (2022, September 26). Interpol issues red notice for fugitive Terra's Do Kwon: South Korea. *Bloomberg.com.* https://www.bloomberg.com/news/articles/2022-09-26/south-korea-says-interpol-issued-red-notice-for-terra-s-do-kwon?leadSource=uverify%20wall

9. *View red notices.* (n.d.). View and search public Red Notices for wanted persons. Interpol.https://www.interpol.int/en/How-we-work/Notices/Red-Notices/View-Red-Notices

10. Osipovich, A. (2022, October 29). Stock Market Today: Dow Closes 800 Points Higher On Inflation Data; Twitter Shares Suspended After Elon Musk Takeover. *WSJ*. https://www.wsj.com/livecoverage/stock-market-news-today-10-28-2022/card/do-kwon-s-other-legal-headache-a-57-million-fraud-lawsuit-in-singapore-5Ix58bBezltt5E95tTI2

11. https://twitter.com/filip_adzic/status/1638886164118802432

1. Vijesti. (2023, March 23). Jedan od najtraženijih bjegunaca i još jedan državljanin Južne Koreje uhapšeni u Crnoj Gori: Upotrijebili lažn. *vijesti.me*. https://www.vijesti.me/vijesti/crna-hronika/649046/jedan-od-najtrazenijih-bjegunaca-i-jos-jedan-drzavljanin-juzne-koreje-uhapseni-u-crnoj-gori-upotrijebili-lazne-isprave

2. Lindrea, B. (2023, March 23). Do Kwon faces fraud charges from US prosecutors hours after arrest. *Cointelegraph*. https://cointelegraph.com/news/do-kwon-faces-fraud-charges-from-us-prosecutors-hours-after-arrest

3. Redman, J. (2022, November 4). *Report: South Korean Prosecutors Accuse Do Kwon of Manipulating LUNA's Market Price.* Bitcoin News. https://news.bitcoin.com/report-south-korean-prosecutors-accuse-do-kwon-of-manipulating-lunas-market-price/

4. *SEC.gov | SEC Charges Terraform and CEO Do Kwon with Defrauding Investors in Crypto Schemes.* (2023, February 16). https://www.sec.gov/news/press-release/2023-32

CRYPTORIES WITH JAVED
THE VIDEO ANIMATOR
MISSED 8 OF
10 ATTEMPTS
TO RECOVER
BITCOINS
7002

STORY 14

149

THE VIDEO ANIMATOR MISSED 8 OF 10 ATTEMPTS TO RECOVER 7,002 BITCOINS

The leading websites, New York Times (1)[1], Guardian (2)[2], Telegraph (3)[3] , BBC (4)[4] etc., published a story on January 12, 2021, about the software developer who is also a video animator. He received 7,002 bitcoins from a client to create an animated video. Unfortunately, he couldn't cash Bitcoin despite his efforts and lost $220 million.

His name is Thomas Stephen. He is a German-born American programmer and a video animator living in San Francisco, USA. He had a small hard drive called Iron Key. Thomas wrote the password of his hard drive on a piece of paper he forgot. Consequently, He could not unlock IronKey, which contained the private keys for a digital wallet of 7,002 bitcoins. So he could not receive millions of dollars worth of bitcoins.

If you forget your Bitcoin hard drive password, you will lose your Bitcoins forever. Traditional banks like Wells Fargo or financial companies like PayPal offer accessible facilities for people to reset their passwords and access their accounts if they forget them.

While Bitcoin has no company that centrally controls it or can reset its password. The creator of Bitcoin, Satoshi Nakamoto, has devised a technology that allows every person in the world to create their own digital bank account where they own their own money without interference from banks and governments.

---

1. https://www.nytimes.com/2021/01/12/technology/bitcoin-passwords-wallets-fortunes.html

2. https://www.theguardian.com/technology/2021/jan/12/in-bits-the-programmer-locked-out-of-his-130m-bitcoin-account

3. https://www.telegraph.co.uk/news/2021/01/12/bitcoin-owner-has-two-guesses-left-unlock-220m-cryptocurrency/

4. https://www.bbc.com/news/technology-55645408

When and where did Stephen get such a large number of bitcoins?

An entrepreneur gave Thomas 7002 bitcoins (3)[1] in 2011 to make an animated video. In those days, the value of bitcoins was minimal.

A maximum of ten attempts can be made to open this drive, and Stephen has failed eight times. Now he has two last chances to get it. If the video animator fails two more times, he will lose hundreds of millions of dollars forever.

---

1. https://www.telegraph.co.uk/news/2021/01/12/bitcoin-owner-has-two-guesses-left-unlock-220m-cryptocurrency/

What is Bitcoin?

Bitcoin is a virtual cryptographic currency. The Bitcoin software is based on the principle of cryptography. Cryptography is a procedure of using coding information intended to protect transactions or data messages in the network. Using cryptographic algorithms, it secures and verifies transactions on its network. Computer networks govern it. The software contains complex algorithms that generate addresses and associated private keys known only to the person who created the Bitcoin wallet.

Users can transfer, store, or withdraw Bitcoin from their digital wallet using the private key. If a user forgets his private key, he can never access his funds.

What thoughts does Stephen express about his loss?

Stephen says he sometimes thinks about his significant loss when he lies in bed at night. He feels sad when the price of Bitcoin keeps increasing, and he owns millions of dollar worth of bitcoins, but he cannot access them. Since he has lost everything, he doesn't want to remember his loss every day.

What is the difference between a Hard drive Password and Private Keys?

A hard drive password lets you access your digital wallet-contained bitcoins. In contrast, the private key (5)[1] is used to authorize your cryptocurrency transactions. Your wallet generates your private key and uses it to generate your public key (your wallet address) through encryption.

Encryption is converting information into a code to prevent unauthorized access. In cryptocurrency, encryption is used to secure and protect private keys and transactions on the network.

---

1. https://www.investopedia.com/terms/p/private-key.asp

Do people often forget their Bitcoin private keys?

Yes. 20 percent (3)[1] of the 18.5 million bitcoins worth $122 billion have gone missing, according to a research report by cryptocurrency data firm Channelalysis. Most people forget their private keys, making accessing their crypto wallet impossible. While some people pass away and keep their wallet information hidden, their families lose out on cryptocurrency.

A similar incident (1)[2] happened to Gabriel Abed, a thirty-four-year-old man from Barbados. In 2011, his friend formatted Gabriel's laptop in which he kept the private key to his 800 bitcoins, due to which he lost his assets of millions of dollars forever.

Gabriel couldn't open an account in a US bank, access a credit card, or use PayPal in the area where he lived. By losing the private key, he has lost his Bitcoins. Today, he could have purchased a 100-acre plot of land in Barbados if he had the cryptocurrency, he bought in 2011 for only a few dollars.

---

1. https://www.telegraph.co.uk/news/2021/01/12/bitcoin-owner-has-two-guesses-left-unlock-220m-cryptocurrency/

2. https://www.nytimes.com/2021/01/12/technology/bitcoin-passwords-wallets-fortunes.html

The Moral of the Story:

Users have lost hundreds of bitcoins due to improperly saving their private keys. Many companies have lost their data through a bug in the system.

People generally use hard drives like USB drives to keep private keys, but their security is also essential. Similarly, users must be careful to protect their passwords. A small carelessness can become a lifelong regret.

References:

1. Popper, N. (2021, Jan.12). Lost Passwords Lock Millionaires Out of Their Bitcoin Fortunes.https://www.nytimes.com/2021/01/12/technology/bitcoin-passwords-wallets-fortunes.html

2. Neate, R. (2021, January 12). Programmer has two guesses left to access £175m bitcoin wallet. *The Guardian*. https://www.theguardian.com/technology/2021/jan/12/in-bits-the-programmer-locked-out-of-his-130m-bitcoin-account

3. The Telegraph. (2021, January 12). Bitcoin owner has only two guesses left to unlock $220m in cryptocurrency. *The Telegraph*. https://www.telegraph.co.uk/news/2021/01/12/bitcoin-owner-has-two-guesses-left-unlock-220m-cryptocurrency/

4. BBC News. (2021, January 13). Man has two guesses to unlock bitcoin worth $240m. *BBC News*. https://www.bbc.com/news/technology-55645408

5. Frankenfield, J. (2023, February 17). *Private Key: What it is, how it works, best ways to store*. Investopedia. https://www.investopedia.com/terms/p/private-key.asp

FROM
VILLIAN
TO HERO
CRYPTORIES WITH JAVED
HOW THE HACKER
RETURNS MILLIONS
OF DOLLARS
WORTH OF STOLEN
CRYPTOCURRENCIES

STORY 15

FROM VILLAIN TO HERO: HOW A HACKER RETURNS MILLIONS OF DOLLARS WORTH OF STOLEN CRYPTOCURRENCIES

This is the story of a hacker who went from Villain to Hero, but to become a hero, he had to become a thief first.

A hacker stole $611 million (1)[1] in cryptocurrency from the Poly network (2)[2] on August 10, 2021. A bug in the system or a weakness in the system's security allowed him to commit this theft on the PolyNetwork DeFi platform.

PolyNetwork is a blockchain-based platform. People can exchange tokens across multiple blockchains, including popular cryptocurrencies like Bitcoin and Ethereum.

CipherTrace, a crypto-intelligence company, considers the attack on the DefiPoly network to be the world's largest attack, and two major incidents have taken place before it, the largest of which was the attack on Tokyo-based exchange Coincheck in 2018, 530 million dollars worth of crypto was stolen. Another crypto theft occurred in 2014 at MTGox in Tokyo, where 850,000 bitcoins were stolen. Globally, it is considered the most prominent Bitcoin theft.

1.   https://www.businesstoday.in/crypto/story/biggest-crypto-heist-hackers-steal-611-million-from-poly-network-return-some-money-after-request-303917-2021-08-11

2.   https://twitter.com/PolyNetwork2/status/1425123153009803267

What makes this theft different from others?

This theft is very different from others in its nature. In his theft, the thief did not intend to obtain the currency illegally but to alert the Poly Network's management about the system's weakness.

The hacker claimed that he didn't want to cause panic in the crypto world, so he targeted Bitcoin and Ether without targeting Dodge Coin in a Q&A post on the Ethereum blockchain. He also said he had always intended to return the currency and was not interested in money.

After this hacking attack, what was the reaction of the public?

An interesting series of messages followed the hacking attack. After the hacker stole the funds, many people congratulated and asked for help. Someone asked for help dealing with the problematic situation due to COVID-19; someone said he has no parents and is responsible for supporting his sisters. As a result, people surrounded by various problems began asking the hacker for help.

In what ways did the company deal with the hacker?

The hacker continued to pay back the money slowly. Poly Network decided not to seek legal action against him but instead honored him, gave him the title of Mr White Hat hacker (3)[1], and offered him a job as its Chief Security Advisor. Additionally, the company offered him a $500,000 Bug Bounty, which he declined.

The Poly Network rewards a bug bounty to a friendly hacker for identifying a security flaw in the software, whereas a white hat means an ethical hacker who identifies system vulnerabilities.

---

1. https://www.cnbc.com/2021/08/23/poly-network-hacker-returns-remaining-cryptocurrency.html#_853ae90f0351324bd73ea615e6487517__4c761f170e016836ff84498202b99827__853ae90f0351324bd73ea615e6487517_text_43ec3e5dee6e706af7766fffea512721_Hacker_0bcef9c45bd8a48eda1b26eb0c61c869_20behind_0bcef9c45bd8a48eda1b26eb0c61c869_20_0bcef9c45bd8a48eda1b26eb0c61c869_24600_0bcef9c45bd8a48eda1b26eb0c61c869_20million_0bcef9c45bd8a48eda1b26eb0c61c869_20crypto_0bcef9c45bd8a48eda1b26eb0c61c869_20heist_0bcef9c45bd8a48eda1b26eb0c61c869_20returns_0bcef9c45bd8a48eda1b26eb0c61c869_20final_0bcef9c45bd8a48eda1b26eb0c61c869_20slice_0bcef9c45bd8a48eda1b26eb0c61c869_20of_0bcef9c45bd8a48eda1b26eb0c61c869_20stolen_0bcef9c45bd8a48eda1b26eb0c61c869_20funds_c0cb5f0fcf239ab3d9c1fcd31fff1efc_-Published_0bcef9c45bd8a48eda1b26eb0c61c869_20Mon_0bcef9c45bd8a48eda1b26eb0c61c869_2C_0bcef9c45bd8a48eda1b26eb0c61c869_20Aug_6cff047854f19ac2aa52aac51bf3af4a_text_43ec3e5dee6e706af7766fffea512721_Cryptocurrency_0bcef9c45bd8a48eda1b26eb0c61c869_20platform_0bcef9c45bd8a48eda1b26eb0c61c869_20Poly_0bcef9c45bd8a48eda1b26eb0c61c869_20Network_0bcef9c45bd8a48eda1b26eb0c61c869_20was_c0cb5f0fcf239ab3d9c1fcd31fff1efc_nearly_0bcef9c45bd8a48eda1b26eb0c61c869_20all_0bcef9c45bd8a48eda1b26eb0c61c869_20of_0bcef9c45bd8a48eda1b26eb0c61c869_20the_0bcef9c45bd8a48eda1b26eb0c61c869_20money.

The company also thanked White Hat for pointing out flaws in the security system. They said that they had solved the platform's security issue.

How much money was stolen by the hacker, and how did he return to the company?

According to The Business Today, the attacker stole (1)[1] $273 million in Ethereum tokens, $253 million in Binance SmartChain tokens, and $85 million in USDC tokens over the Polygon network. The total worth of stolen Ether, Binance tokens, and USDC tokens was equivalent to 611 million dollars.

Initially, the Polyhacker returned assets in parts, then contacted the company on August 23, 2021, and provided a private key for transferring the remaining funds (4)[2].

There is no evidence found that either Mr. White Hat accepted the bug bounty or the job offer.

---

1. https://www.businesstoday.in/crypto/story/biggest-crypto-heist-hackers-steal-611-million-from-poly-network-return-some-money-after-request-303917-2021-08-11

2.   https://medium.com/poly-network/poly-network-commences-full-asset-restoration-7f5c548423b9

The Crux of the Story:

It is a strange incident of its kind in which a thief succeeds in stealing millions of dollars. He could have lived comfortably with that money if he wanted. Actually, he was not a thief but a custodian of people's money who not only returned the crypto assets worth a tremendous amount but pointed out the poor security system of the exchange. The incident highlighted the risks of unregulated security in the system and drew crypto regulators' attention.

References:

1. Kaur, A. (2021, August 11). Biggest crypto heist! Hackers steal $611 million from Poly Network; return some money after request. Business Today. https://www.businesstoday.in/crypto/story/biggest-crypto-heist-hackers-steal-611-million-from-poly-network-return-some-money-after-request-303917-2021-08-11

2. https://twitter.com/PolyNetwork2/status/1425123153009803267

3. Browne, R. (2021, August 24). Hacker behind $600 million crypto heist returns final slice of stolen funds. CNBC. https://www.cnbc.com/2021/08/23/poly-network-hacker-returns-remaining-cryptocurrency.html

4. Poly Network. (2022, August 23). Poly Network commences full asset restoration - Poly Network - medium. Medium. https://medium.com/poly-network/poly-network-commences-full-asset-restoration-7f5c548423b9

Acknowledgement

I am the real author of this book, and I only edited, refined and proofread the text with the help of AI-based tools.

I am grateful to my sincere friend **Ghalib Shamim** (KSA) who has been very supportive in my life. I am also thankful to my true friend **Dr. Nighat Shaheen** (USA) for taking excellent care of my mother, as if she were her own mother.

I would like to express my gratitude to my mentor, **Prof. Dr. Olivier Hance**, owner of the Hance Law Firm (Luxembourg). His constructive feedback was instrumental in refining my ideas during the writing process.

I acknowledge the moral support received from my family members in writing the manuscript.

All my success belongs to my beloved Aunty (late) **Syeda Abida Perveen** and my Uncle **Sultan Sikandar**, who raised me.

Furthermore, KDP Amazon makes self-publishing easy and affordable, which is greatly appreciated.

Thank you **all** for choosing my book and letting me share crypto stories with you. I hope reading it will be as enjoyable as writing it.

Javed Iqbal
March 04, 2024

Disclaimer

I am not a financial advisor and that none of the content of this book is investment advice but rather a narration of real stories and my opinion. You should consult with a financial consultant or do your own research. Neither the publisher nor the author shall be liable for any loss or any other damages.